FINI
AFTER 50

#4-

COPY

To Charlie & JoAnne,

How to Begin

meeting 6/28/02

Where to Go

An uncommon love.

What to Do

Tom Blake

By
Tom Blake

Tooter's Publishing
Dana Point, California

Copyright © 2003 by Tom Blake

Finding Love After 50
How to Begin. Where to Go. What to Do

Edited by Frances P. Blake, Greta Cohn and Tammy Lutz

Library of Congress Control Number: 2003091468
ISBN 0-9727966-0-6

To order this book, e-mail TPBlake@aol.com or call (949) 248-9008. Visa, Mastercard or checks accepted. For your convenience, an order form is on page 159.

Although the author and publisher have exhaustively researched all sources to ensure the accuracy and completeness of the information contained in this book, they assume no responsibility for errors, inaccuracies, misquotes, omissions, or any inconsistency herein. Any slights of people or organizations are unintentional.

Printed in the United States by

Morris Publishing
3212 East Highway 30
Kearney, NE 68847
1-800 650-7888

DEDICATION

A Special Moment

My mom, Fran Blake, was widowed 37 years ago. She's had opportunities to remarry, but she felt her quality of life would be better by remaining single. She lives in a wonderful retirement community called Oakmont, which is located among the vineyards, in the Valley of the Moon, between Sonoma and Santa Rosa, California.

Last year, Mom wanted a new car. My life partner, Greta Cohn, and I drove Mom to a car dealer in South San Francisco. When the salesman handed her the purchase contract to sign, Mom asked me to review it first.

Of course, sons know how old their moms are. And I most certainly know, because I was born on Mom's birthday, November 11. But when I saw "Age of Buyer: *91 years*," on the contract, I was reminded of how blessed my family--brother Bill, sisters, Pam and Chris, and I--are to have a mom so vital and so precious.

I believe the keys to Mom's longevity are a positive attitude, exercise and keeping her mind active by reading, doing crosswords and playing bridge (she helped edit this book). But, most important: *she loves people and being out with them.* As you read this book, remember this important point—if singles want to enrich their lives, and increase their chances of meeting a new partner, they need to be out with people, just like my mom is.

This book is dedicated to Frances Pardee Blake, who, at 92, can be seen driving around Oakmont in her white Volkswagen Golf. She's an inspiration to all.

Contents

Acknowledgments

I wish to thank the readers of my newspaper columns--many from all over the United States, some from foreign countries, but mainly the residents of Orange County, California--who have contributed information since the columns began in 1994. It takes guts to back up your opinions and comments with your name in the paper.

Thanks to my Mom, Fran Blake, of Santa Rosa, Calif., and Tammy Lutz, my friend of Dana Point, Calif., for editing the book.

To George Mair, Dana Point, author extraordinaire, friend for 23 years, for being my writing mentor and for encouraging me to keep writing.

To Mark Victor Hansen, Newport Beach, for the quote on the front cover of this book and for helping millions of people with his upbeat and positive outlook on life.

To Teresa and Rosa, my loyal employees for 16 years, who made it possible for me to leave Tutor and Spunky's Deli in their hands, while I took time off to write.

To my family—Mom, Bill, Pam, Chris, Bob, Linda, Derek and Rod—for your love and caring.

And to Greta Cohn, my life partner, for her keen editing eye, and who has brought peace and happiness to my life, with her encouragement, positive attitude and outlook on life, demeanor, kindness and love of children and mankind. I'm a lucky man.

Introduction

This book's goal is simple: to help middle-aged and older singles improve their chances of meeting someone special, and to revitalize their lives at the same time.

On Christmas Eve, 1993, my wife of six years backed up a truck to the front door of our home, took what furniture and belongings she wanted and moved out of my life. Normally, married couples would discuss an event of this magnitude beforehand, but I was left out of the loop, and you can imagine my shock when I came home to a nearly-empty house. Christmas wasn't merry that year. And just like that, at age 53, I joined a large group of men and women--middle aged and older—who find themselves single.

After the initial few weeks of clearing my head and getting my life somewhat in order (and checking out garage sales to replenish the furniture), I decided to date.

I thought dating would be easy--I'm a fairly outgoing guy and I own Tutor and Spunky's Deli on Pacific Coast Highway in Dana Point, Calif., where lots of single women have lunch. But, new singles do foolish things because they're lonely and I was no exception. The scenario went like this.

Single woman in deli: "I'll have a vegetarian sandwich on wheat bread, extra sprouts, hold the mayo and cheese."

Deli proprietor (me): (Without giving her a chance to order a beverage or even get out her wallet) "Would you like to have dinner tonight?"

She'd look at me as if I were nuts. I'm surprised I didn't drive every single woman customer away. Thankfully, I

came to my senses and stopped asking customers out.
I realized I wasn't prepared to date. I didn't know how to begin, where to go or what to do.

As I made my way through the dating maze, I wrote my experiences in a journal, describing good dates, bad dates, blind dates, getting stood up, rejected and dumped, not getting enough sleep, spending too much money, drinking too much red wine and eating far too much pasta.

After five months of searching for the perfect woman, I decided to stay home one night to rest. Over the next three weeks, I converted the journal notes into a 75-page story about my roller-coaster life since Xmas Eve.

Eventually, those pages became the basis for a newspaper column called *Middle Aged and Dating Again*. Two women editors at the *Dana Point News*--my local newspaper--figured women would enjoy reading about the pathetic dating exploits of a pathetic single man. The column is now syndicated.

I've written more than 500 newspaper and online columns about middle-age dating and relationships. The columns led to a book--also called *Middle Aged and Dating Again*. A separate column called *Single Again* appears in *The Orange County Register*, the 22nd largest newspaper in the United States.

The 2000 Census revealed there are nearly 29,000,000 Americans over the age of 50 living alone and that number is growing. Over 10,000 baby boomers turn 50 every day, half of them single. The divorce rate for first marriages exceeds 50 per cent, for second and third marriages, 70 per cent. Large numbers of people over age 50 are single, facing life alone. For most of them, it's sad and scary.

Most older singles cope well, but they're lonely. If they had a choice, they'd like to have a mate again, but they're lost--as I was--with little idea of how to proceed.

They seek information on how to find a mate, but little has been written for the older set. And most of what's been written--no offense intended--has been written by women. That's good, women relate to women. But women tell me they want to learn about the man's perspective on middle-age dating, and there's not much information available from the man's point-of-view.

I'm not a therapist, psychologist, or marriage counselor. No doctorate degree in failed relationships, but plenty of experience with them. Just a regular middle-aged guy who's been divorced three times and survived to date again, and who, over nine years of writing columns, has received comments, stories, woes, questions, and tears, from thousands of readers. I understand what the 29,000,000 older singles are going through.

I've gathered the most valuable and useful information from readers and condensed it into the pages of this book. I've tried to keep it simple and brief. No gimmicks. No rules. No idealistic stuff. My premise is that middle-aged singles are intelligent and don't want to be embarrassed, so I won't recommend anything demeaning for them to do.

As you read this book, there are no guarantees that you'll find someone, but you'll be making an educated effort, and improving your chances. More importantly, you'll be on the road to enriching your life. Some readers will meet a mate as a result of something they learned from within the book's pages.

The book is primarily for women, but men will learn

from it also, as will younger singles. Married couples will enjoy the book. Many tell me they read my columns because the messages help them appreciate their spouses more. Some married people will purchase the book because they know or suspect their marital status will be changing soon. Widows tell me my columns have helped them through the difficult times and have given them information and hope. Adult children will purchase the book for their single parents, hoping to help their parents overcome their loneliness and being alone.

My e-mail address is TPBlake@aol.com. I hope you'll let me know how you feel about what you've read.

Chapter 1

Answering Matt Lauer's Question

We always believe that love is forever. I guess forever doesn't last as long as it used to

--Column reader Bill, reflecting on the end of his marriage

During my second appearance on the *Today* show, Matt Lauer asked, "Why is dating after 50 so difficult?"

I smiled, hesitated and said, "Matt, some of us haven't had a date in 30 years. We're out of practice."

Of course, there are more answers to Matt's question than that. There are five main reasons why dating after 50 is so difficult. It's important singles understand them so they'll stop blaming themselves for being so perplexed.

1. We aren't prepared

Our generation has had a trick played on it. Most of us believed we'd retire with our spouses, enjoy the golden years together and that's what we prepared for.

But for millions of us, life hasn't worked out that way. Instead of being married at middle age, we're single. Our spouse is gone. He may have passed away or run away (with his secretary or a younger woman, the rat). Whether we're widowed or divorced, we're alone--in a situation we never thought we'd be in--and we're not prepared for it.

Most of us would like to share our lives with someone again, so we decide to look for a new partner. But, it's been years since our last date. We don't know where to begin. We have many questions but few answers: How to begin? Where to go? What to do? Whom to date? Where to meet him? How to act? Where to find information? (There isn't much available for older singles.) This book answers those questions and hundreds more. It will help prepare you for finding a mate.

2. There aren't places to go where there are even numbers of single men and women

When we were in high school, college, or even after we graduated, meeting singles to date was easy. There were parties, dances, football games, study hall—lots of places to meet other singles our age.

But, now that we're older, it's harder to meet singles because there are so few places where they congregate in even numbers of both sexes. It's too bad there aren't big barns or halls where singles over 50 could go. You'd just walk up to the appropriate table and sign up. I would go to the table marked: *Male 60-65, seeking compatible female*. But those types of places don't exist.

Hence, to meet other singles, we need to venture outside our normal routines and go places we haven't considered before.

3. We've aged

Many of us are still working. When we come home at night, we're tired. The last thing we feel like doing is getting cleaned up to go out on a date, perhaps with a stranger we don't know. We'd rather plop down on the couch and enjoy a glass of wine. We hit the sack early because we don't sleep as well as before. We don't have the energy we used to have. And dating takes energy (and time, and money).

Also, we have a few lines in our faces, we've gained some pounds and we get new aches and pains in the damnedest places. We creak when we walk. We think we're not as attractive or healthy as we once were. Our confidence may be iffy. We're afraid we won't measure up, and we fear rejection. Dating is intimidating now that we're older.

4. How do we find somebody compatible?

I'm finding it difficult to meet someone who doesn't have a lot of insecurities and fears in their later years. I can't seem to reassure them that I am NOT after their money or their possessions. It's so frustrating.

--Robin Nugent, Buena Park, Calif.

Let's say we've managed to put ourselves out there, we've had a few dates. Unfortunately, the task has just begun. The next hurdle: finding someone compatible, a person who thinks as we think, has similar values, interests and energy levels, is somewhat close to our age, and who appeals to us physically. As if that's not enough, they have to feel the same way about us. With all of these constraints, no wonder finding a compatible mate is difficult. How do we find that gem amid the pile of rocks?

Not to mention, as we grow older, we're more demanding and set in our ways. We've experienced life, we know what we want and what works for us. We're wiser. We're not going to accept someone (at least we shouldn't) to share our life who doesn't measure up. As we

3

add each requirement to our list, the pool of available people suitable for us shrinks.

5. Dating after 50 is more difficult for women

When I was a young girl in Texas, I couldn't have imagined I would end up alone in my 50s!

---A Laguna Beach, Calif., lawyer

The fifth reason dating after 50 is difficult applies only to women. They've had an even bigger trick played on them. For women, meeting men is harder by the numbers alone. Why? Because statistics favor men.

A woman named Marilyn approached me after a speech to a group of seniors at a community center in Mission Viejo, Calif. She said, "It's pretty discouraging when you go to a social function and there are fifteen women and one man. I believe a personal introduction through other means has a better chance than at these functions."

Marilyn's right on both issues. A 15:1 ratio (or even half that) is discouraging for women (probably even for the poor guy, who likely feels overwhelmed and may be seen disappearing through the side exit door). Getting to know an available single man at a function like that is nearly impossible. And, as Marilyn said, there are better ways to meet a potential mate than attending an event where there are so few men.

Here are some statistics to ponder about the U.S. population. I'm not presenting these to discourage women, but to explain the realities of the numbers women are up against. When you realize that an important reason you haven't met a man is because the numbers are against you--that it has little to do with you-- accepting the situation should be easier.

Statistics to ponder

- At age 45, there are 2.47 single women for each divorced or widowed man
- At age 65, 45 per cent of the women are widows, outnumbering widowers by nearly 5 to 1
- At age 70, the ratio of single women to single men is somewhere around 6:1

And, women are quick to point out that these ratios don't capture the true picture. They say that many of those men aren't relationship material and rattle off a long list of reasons why: Men don't date or go to social events, they're too set in their ways, too lazy, (around retirement communities, women say that all these geezers want is a nurse and a purse), they want women to wait on them, all they want is sex, and many are only interested in dating younger women (we tackle that *hot topic* in Chapter 8).

Yet, there are more than 9,000,000 unmarried men over age 50 in the United States who are potential mates. Not enough to go around, but still a large number.

At an AARP convention, I heard a woman reporter say to Dr. Ruth Westheimer, "I can't meet single men. Where are they hiding?"

Dr. Ruth gave the best answer I've ever heard about the shortage of quality men. She said, "The ratio is a fact of life, you can't change it. However, if you put your mind to having a nice appearance, and an openness to meeting new people, and a willingness to do social things, and you're positive, you can effectively reduce the ratio."

Dr. Ruth also told the woman to acknowledge the ratios, but not to dwell on them, nor to make excuses because of them. Then, she told the woman to commit to having a good life, with or without a man.

Now that we understand why dating after 50 is difficult, we need to get out in the world and make the best of it. In the next chapter, we look at seven initial steps that will help make dating after 50 easier.

Chapter 2

Seven Steps To Get You Started

To improve your chances of meeting a mate, you need to get active and follow these seven initial steps.

1. Get off the couch and out of the house

Taking this first step is crucial. You may not feel like venturing out, staying home is more comfortable. We've acknowledged that dating takes time and energy. But no one is going to knock on your door to ask you out. So, it's either get off the couch and get out, or stay at home and be lonely.

Your life has changed, and you need to change. You may live for another 50 years, you might as well try to enjoy them. By getting out, you'll find a purpose in living, you'll feel better about yourself and you'll be on the road to enriching your life.

2. Get off the pity pot and be positive

Nine years ago, when I first started writing my newspaper columns, hardly a column went by when I didn't mention my wife leaving on Xmas Eve. Woe-was-me. I wrote about how unfair I'd been treated. A woman reader wrote: "Get off the pity pot! You're whining too much. Put your wife's leaving behind you, move on and take us readers with you. We want action and advice, romance, excitement. Give us dating information without the crying towel."

I thought she was being too harsh at the time, but in retrospect, she was right.

When we lose a mate--from death, divorce or a breakup--it's devastating. Friends rally around us. They're there for us and hold our hand during the difficult times. We're hurt and have big holes in our hearts. That's natural and understandable.

But, there comes a time when friends (and newspaper column readers) feel they've heard enough. They expect to see signs of healing. They want us to mend and get on with life. They want us to smile and be positive.

This pity-pot alert also applies to complaining about the opposite sex. Stuff like there aren't enough men and all the good ones are taken, and the rest of the reasons mentioned in the last chapter. Closely related to this is "gender bashing." See item six below.

After healing, we need to stop whining and feeling sorry for ourselves. We need to realize that things are the way they are, and to make the best of them. So get off the pity-pot, and adopt a positive attitude. Having the latter is important in dating, and even more so in life.

3. Billy Crystal was right

In the movie, *Forget Paris,* Billy Crystal fell in love with an American woman in Paris. When he found out she was married, he said to her: "Don't make yourself available if you aren't available."

After the loss of a relationship, many people--because they're lonely--put themselves on the dating block too soon, as the next story illustrates.

I have an author friend named George Mair. To celebrate the release of his book, "Excelsior! The Amazing Life of Stan Lee," which George co-authored with Stan (the creator of Spider Man), George invited a new divorcee on a blind date.

As they were sipping glasses of wine, and getting to know each other, George observed that the woman couldn't stop talking about her ex-husband Harry. She droned on and on. She never asked George about George. He felt he could have left the table and she wouldn't have noticed (until the bill came).

George is a gentleman, so instead of leaving, he said to the cocktail server, "Three more."

"Why the third glass?" the grieving woman asked.

"There's one for you, of course, and one for me, and one for Harry. You've talked so much about him, I feel I know him as a friend, and if he comes walking through that door and pulls up a chair, I want him to feel welcome."

George and the woman didn't go out again. Of course, the point of the story is, if people are still grieving the loss of a loved one, it's too early for them to be dating. They aren't mentally available. A married person is not available. Be sure you're available, and the person you're dating is also. Which leads us to the next item, the importance of healing a broken heart before trying to force someone new into it.

4. Heal First

Losing a loved one is devastating. It disables us. People suffering a loss may need to seek professional help from a grief counselor or therapist. Dealing with the loss of losing someone goes far beyond the scope of this book. AARP has a valuable website, http://www.aarp.org/griefandloss/ for people who are having trouble dealing with their loss. It has all kinds of resources. Or, if a person needs to talk, trained AARP volunteers answer a toll free line, 1-866-797-2277, daily, 9 a.m. to 9 p.m., Eastern time.

John Gray, in his book *Mars and Venus Starting Over,* discusses the four critical stages of healing after a loss. Gray states that people need to properly heal before they can successfully open their hearts and love again. That's important advice. I recommend anyone who has suffered a loss read *Mars and Venus Starting Over.*

Barbara Gilvary, Laguna Hills, Calif., said, "The best thing my husband did for me in 38 years was leave me. I have become, or at least am on my way to becoming spiritually healthy. I have been able to help people who are facing what I faced 5 years ago, because I have walked in their shoes. I tell them that before they go out looking for a mate, get to know themselves. The real connection is the connection with self. We look for another human being to fill up that part of ourselves that is missing. It's only after we feel whole, with no missing parts, that we will be able to share love with another person."

One of my readers wrote, "You'll know you're ready to date when you no longer find dwelling on the past comforting. Only you will know when you're ready."

5. The Mental Preparedness Test

Here's a simple, fun test, to determine if you're mentally available to date. It's not scientific, only an indication of whether you're ready.

Answer the ten questions. Don't zip through them, think about each one and be honest. Don't fudge to get a high score, there are no right or wrong answers.

Circle each number you can say "yes" to

1. My broken heart has healed. I don't think about my ex every waking minute any more

2. I'll set aside time and money to date

3. I will trust and open my heart

4. I'll get out of the house and pursue new activities

5. I will openly and honestly communicate

6. I won't take rejection personally or get discouraged

7. I'll keep an open mind about men (women)

8. I'll have a positive attitude

9. My expectations are realistic. Dating is a numbers game. I might not find the right man (woman) for a long time. There are no guarantees

10. I believe there is someone for me

If two or more questions aren't circled, you're likely not ready to date. Wait a couple of months. Do some projects around the house, like painting the laundry room, or reorganizing the garage (again). Time works wonders.

6. Avoid Gender Bashing

I am unattached because men are poor, cheap, not well-spoken or well-read. They're players, cheaters or liars and the pool is very thin.

--a woman with an unhealthy dating attitude

Some women get a pretty raw deal from men (works both ways). It's easy to develop a "man-bashing" attitude, similar to the woman above. When Pearl Hedlund, of San Antonio, Texas, read the above quote, she shared her thoughts. "Wow!! I know why some folks never find anyone to love again. Sure wouldn't want to get involved with that lady—that is, if I were a man."

Pearl's right. When women "bash men," they can kiss their dating careers good-bye, because men don't want to hear it, and won't tolerate it.

The same goes for men. Some are bitter and think women are guilty of every evil under the sun. The men feel they got screwed everyway to Friday and back in their divorces and consequently "bash women." Women will avoid them like a clove of raw garlic.

Dating after 50 has no spot for bashing the opposite sex. That's negative behavior, and to date successfully, men and women need to zip their critical lips and be positive.

7. Network every chance you get

What's the least expensive and most effective way of finding someone who might be right for you? Networking.

Networking is simply letting everyone you know that you're available and would enjoy meeting potential people to date. Tell your friends, co-workers and relatives. Mention it to your buddy, the produce manager of the local market, or the post office front desk clerk. And don't do it just one time and let it drop. Life changes. That gentleman you thought was so nice at the neighborhood Christmas party (who had a girlfriend) may not have a girlfriend now. So remind the people you've told before you're still in the market. Of course, don't be such a pest that you come off as desperate.

Rebecca spent $4000 on a dating service. She had a few so-so dates, but no one clicked. Then, her neighbor, who had taken it upon herself to help Rebecca, noticed a new single man had moved in a block away. She dragged Rebecca down to meet him. Rebecca and the man married six months later.

Sometimes, your friends know the type of person who would be good for you better than you know yourself. Not all introductions via networking work out, but your chances of meeting somebody compatible are greater than when meeting strangers via the internet or even through a dating service.

Follow the seven steps in this chapter—get off the couch and out of the house, get off the pity pot and be positive, be sure you're mentally available, heal your broken heart before dating, take *The Mental Preparedness Test* (not too seriously, though), don't bash the opposite sex and network constantly. Implement these suggestions and you'll be on your way to dating success.

Chapter 3

Seven Tips to Make Dating Easier

In this chapter, seven tips are presented that will make middle age dating easier. The first two are simple to implement, and yet can work wonders in meeting men.

1. Be approachable

To improve your chances of meeting a mate, you must be approachable. The common thread of approachability is simply friendliness and a smile. Being friendly means you're receptive and interested. A smile says, "I'd enjoy meeting you." If people are shy, they may come off as unapproachable, even though they'd like to be approached. My friend Jackie, a customer in my deli, is a good example.

Jackie's not her real name. I call her that because she reminds me of Jackie Kennedy. Not only does she look like Jackie, but she has the same charming mannerisms.

Jackie told me that one day after her divorce six years ago, she was with her son in the boy's clothing section at K-Mart. She noticed an attractive man, also with his young son. "The man was giving me 'the look,'" Jackie said, "and then he smiled warmly as my son and I walked passed him on our way to the cash register."

"What happened?" I asked, anticipating a we-met-by-fate story.

"Nothing, at least not then." There was more to be told.

"Five years later, a similar thing happened, only this time, in the parking lot of another store. As I was loading a box into my trunk, a man was staring at me, as he was loading a box into his SUV. Again, it was 'the look,' and the same man."

I was excited. Jackie had a second chance at meeting the man of her dreams. As a columnist always looking for romance success stories, again I asked, "What happened?"

And again Jackie replied, "Nothing. Should I have said something to him?"

I thought about her question for a moment and said, "No, not if you prefer spending another five years alone."

I felt so strongly that Jackie and the man with "the look" were meant for each other, I wrote a column about her story, which included an all-points-bulletin type of plea: if the man should happen to read the column, would he contact me. He didn't and Jackie is still alone. If she had made herself approachable, perhaps the guy would have worked up the courage to introduce himself. Singles, especially women, need to be approachable.

Giselle Blum, of New Orleans, explained how she makes herself approachable: "Find some place where middle-aged and older single men are, even if it's an upscale lounge or a singles dance. Don't go with or talk much to other women. Just sit or stand confidently with a smile or at least not any part of a frown. Watch that your body language isn't a turn off, like crossed arms.

"If you see someone who appeals to you, catch his glance for just a moment (be sure he notices your glance), then look away, keep looking friendly and perhaps in a few minutes give one more quick glance. It's called flirting and it works. Believe that you are attractive and interesting and you're more than half way towards meeting a nice man. It may go no further, but it's a start."

In some cases, being friendly and approachable may not be enough. You may need to take the initiative and be assertive.

2. Be assertive

Women's roles have changed. In the workplace, women have broken through the glass ceiling, not totally, but it's happening.

At home, single moms are finding themselves assuming some of the roles that men used to fill. They raise kids on their own and for the most part do an excellent job of it. Women adjust well to adversity.

But in the dating world, women have been slower to adapt. They remember the old days when men did the asking and paying for dates. That was proper back then and what some women still insist on today.

But, if women want to make finding a mate easier, they need to assume some of the role that men previously filled. They need to be willing to ask a man out, and when they do, they should assume they're going to pay.

Many women throw their arms up in protest. They insist, "That's not the way I was brought up," or, "I'm a lady, I would never ask a man for a date."

I'm not recommending women toss away their ladylike qualities or become piranhas, they just need to become a bit assertive in situations that warrant it. Jackie's situation warranted it. Had she introduced herself to the guy, either time, who knows what would have happened? They obviously had an attraction for each other. At least she wouldn't still be wondering "what if?"

Seven Tips To Make Dating Easier

Meeting potential mates at our age is difficult. When an opportunity to meet someone presents itself, it's likely a one-time occurrence, seldom do we get a chance to meet the same person again. The opportunity is similar to a vacant airplane seat, once it's gone, it's gone. Singles need to be assertive at that moment.

Notice, we're using the word "assertive," not the word "aggressive," which has suggestive overtones. I'm not advocating putting a chain around a guy and dragging him to the bedroom. I'm simply suggesting asking a man if he'd like to meet for coffee sometime. In dating, it's not only okay for women to be assertive, it's wise.

Here's how I was assertive at an A & W Root Beer stand in San Rafael, Calif. I watched a woman (not wearing a wedding ring) who appealed to me sit down to eat a hot dog. I wanted to meet her but didn't have the nerve to approach her. She didn't eat the bun so I asked her if I could have the bun to feed my dog, who was in the car. She said, "Only if I can meet your dog." On the way to the car, she said she was allergic to flour. We dated a few times. Turns out, she was allergic to me.

Cheryl Shisler, Huntington Beach, Calif., said, "The best way to meet people is to start up a conversation. I'm the friendly type. You never know if the next person you start talking to will be the one you've been looking for all along. Take a chance. If a woman, or in my case, a man, is turned off by your pleasant conversation, they aren't the one for you. I met a wonderful man in our local grocery store."

Here's another example of how assertiveness can work. I gave a speech at the AARP national convention in San Diego. Among other points, I stressed what I've written in this chapter about being approachable and assertive. Two weeks after the convention, an anonymous woman sent this letter:

"My friend Ann asked me and another friend to attend your seminar. The two of us are married but went along to support her. She's a beautiful woman with a great personality who has had only one or two dates since the death of her husband nine years ago. She's a little shy because we're from that 'old school' of thought and it's hard for her to make the first move.

"We enjoyed your presentation and were laughing a great deal. A gentleman two rows in front of us turned side ways to catch our reaction. After the presentation, he started a conversation, asking if we were married. The two of us replied yes but said Ann wasn't.

"He said his wife had died four years ago and he had decided to move on and he thought the convention was an excellent place to meet someone near his own age. I replied, 'What about my friend Ann?' He said, "Well, I was waiting for her to say something." A little assertive of me, but you said in your speech, 'don't let a chance pass you by.' And Ann was being very shy.

"They exchanged phone numbers and he asked us to lunch. We went to the remaining sessions together and the next morning he was waiting for us. The two of them went out on a date Saturday night and Sunday and really hit it off. She has returned home to Orange County and he to Michigan, but they have called each other several times and he is coming out to see her next month."

I love that story. It shows when singles get out, even though they aren't looking for a mate, things can happen.

And while Ann wasn't assertive, her friend was, which led to Ann meeting the man.

3. Have "name cards" printed

For shy folks, it's hard to initiate a conversation with a stranger. And this is where a "name card" can be useful. A "name card" has your name or a false name on it and a telephone number or e-mail address where a person can reach you. But, you must protect yourself. If you're listed in the telephone book, use a false name. Have a telephone number that rings into an answering service, where you pick up your messages and only return the calls you want. Don't use your home number or street address. If you use e-mail, don't use your name in the address. The free e-mail services work well for that purpose.

If you see a man you'd like to talk to, give him your "name card" and tell him you'd like him to call you. You can do that even if you're shy. Have a hundred or so printed. They will come in handy.

Being approachable and assertive may lead to rejection, which is discussed next.

4. Don't take rejection personally

It seems most 40-50 year-olds look upon any date that doesn't work out as a rejection. Instead, let's just have fun trying and not put such importance on it. People have different interests and lifestyles and not everybody is going to be compatible. Don't take rejection personally and don't give up because of it.

Duane Marshall, single, Long Beach, Calif.

Rejection is a part of middle-age dating. If Jackie had approached the guy, and he had been married, so what? Duane's right, just chalk it up to the dating deal.

A woman who attended one of my speeches decided to follow my advice about being assertive. She had never asked a man out in her life. She finally worked up the nerve when she saw a guy in a clothing store. He was most gracious but told her he was married. She was horrified and e-mailed me instantly: "I'm never, ever, ever doing that again." She should have just moved on.

5. "A few pounds overweight"

If a woman is any more than a few pounds overweight, she is shunned by the male population. On the Internet, the Love@aol.com profile is a place that asks about your body style. If you're honest and say yes— you're a few pounds overweight--you might as well delete your profile.

--anonymous single woman

Here's a topic that always gets me in trouble. Women get angry at me when I write about losing weight. But, I'd be remiss if I didn't mention the importance of it in dating. The following story illustrates how women take their weight personally.

A married reader sent me an e-mail about her friend Marcy: "My best friend of 35 years needs a good man! Marcy is kind in spirit, funny in words, and a quality person. Can you make any suggestions about where/how to meet a marriage-minded man, for a 49-year-old wonderful woman?"

It was evident the married woman cared about Marcy. We all need friends like that. She ended her e-mail with: "Do all men want 'trophy-like' younger, Barbie-doll women? Or, are there any out there who can see beyond the years of living and having children and seek someone who looks just like they do: normal aging lines, a few pounds overweight, a few aches and pains, but truly, a winning personality full of amenities. Thank you for your guidance for my groovy friend."

I responded: "True, most of us have normal aging lines and aches and pains. But, red flag alert: 'a few pounds overweight.' Your friend should address that. It sounds like she's got everything else to make her quite a catch. To me, 'a few pounds overweight' means she doesn't take care of herself as much as she should, and that could be a concern to a gentleman. Besides, shedding those pounds is a healthy alternative."

Keep in mind, I had never met the woman, and was answering a question about another woman I had never seen. I answer a couple hundred e-mails a week, and don't always keep track of which person sent what.

A few days later, a stranger sent me an *instant message* on AOL. At first, I thought the married woman must have a boyfriend because the *instant message* referred to the married woman as 'my girlfriend.' The sender didn't identify herself and came across as being angry and defensive. Actually, she came on like a charging rhino. I couldn't figure out the connection to the married woman until the message read: "I'm not fat."

Since I was heading out the door, I suggested she e-mail me and we could discuss her beef--or her buns--in a sensible manner. She didn't write back. After her *instant message* interruption, I turned off *instant messaging* forever on my computer.

A few days later, the married woman e-mailed: "Marcy felt you didn't recognize my point...she is quite attractive, has the normal lines of a 49-year-old, and is in good physical shape." (I'm not sure what "the normal lines of a 49-year-old" are.)

The point of the story: women are sensitive about their weight and how they look. Most don't want to hear suggestions about losing weight or getting in shape. They counter that men want women to look good, but the men don't take care of themselves, so why should they.

If you're out of shape or "a few pounds overweight," you'd be better off addressing those issues before you start dating. Enlightened women and men want to date people who take their physical condition and health seriously. Most singles don't want to be with a person who has let himself or herself go. You don't have to be perfect or gorgeous, but you need to get in shape (intensive walking is a great way to begin). Remember the ratios we discussed in chapter 1? It's competitive out there.

People can lose weight. A New Mexico woman said, "Remember those 72 pounds I had gained? I'm happy to say that 40 of them are gone. It's been a lot of work, but I'm feeling great, and guys are starting to notice me. Life is good." This woman knows the importance of being in shape, and while it's a long way back, she's doing it.

A woman named Yolanda e-mailed, "I exercise on almost a daily basis. I'm self-motivated and go by myself to the gym. Those seniors who complain about their health, are stay-at-home people who don't venture out, and don't exercise. I live in an apartment with 33 steps and no elevator. I climb the steps with no problem and I'm over 65. Exercise keeps us agile, gives us a good feeling, keeps us young. From comments I receive from my peers and all with whom I come in contact, I don't look or act my age."

6. Have realistic expectations

This happened to me. I was in New York City on a Saturday night, Upper West Side, looking for a restaurant where some singles might be. I wanted to celebrate with a plate of pasta and a glass of merlot. That morning, I had been interviewed by Jack Ford, live on the *Today* Show, as an expert on dating after 50.

At the corner of 83rd and Amsterdam, I found an Italian restaurant that was teeming with people. I made my way to the only unoccupied barstool. The woman on my left was young, late 20s, attractive. She kept staring at me. She was giving me 'the look' that Jackie described earlier. I wondered if she was looking for a dinner partner.

"Are you a writer?" she asked, as she bit a martini olive.

"Why yes, I am," thinking I must look the part.

"I saw you on the *Today* Show. My name's Stefani."

If my barstool hadn't had big oak legs, I would have tumbled over backwards, right on my rear. Dinner with a nice partner here I come. I wondered, would we eat here, or go someplace more private and secluded?

I'd read somewhere that writers are sexy to women. I didn't believe it, but I'd read it. Here I was in the Big Apple with an attractive younger woman showing an interest because I was a writer who had been on national television that morning, a long way from the reality of making sandwiches in my deli.

Stefani made the next move: "My mother would be perfect for you."

Shot and hit. Deflated. Rejected. But, not showing my disappointment I said, "Why don't we phone your mom and see if she can come over?" I thought 'Mom' might live on Central Park West, and be able to join us in a few minutes.

But 'Mom' lived in West Palm Beach, Florida. Stefani had dinner with a girlfriend and I ate calamari at the bar--by myself. I waddled back to my hotel, the Essex House on Central Park South, reminding myself to practice what I had preached in front of millions of viewers earlier that day: keep your dating expectations realistic. A woman isn't going to be interested in a man when he's 25 to 30 years older (I did exchange e-mails with her mother, but we never got together. Living 3,000 miles apart isn't realistic for developing a relationship).

If you're 50 or 60, and you're a woman hoping for a Tom Cruise look-a-like, or you're a man hoping for Julia Roberts, or you want to date somebody 23-years-younger, you're not being realistic. You'll end up being disappointed and rejected. Older men often seek younger women. In most cases, those men aren't being realistic. The age-difference issue is the topic of Chapter 8.

One woman offered wise advice about realistic expectations. "I think people who date looking for perfection in others miss a world of average everyday people. These are the people who work hard, play hard, love lots, and have so much to give, and are overlooked due to 'lack of perfection.'"

She's right. There are lots of wonderful singles out there who aren't perfect, but would make great mates. Don't look for the perfect person—they probably don't exist, and if they do, they're likely in somebody else's arms. Everyone at our age carries some baggage.

I'm not saying to lower your standards, or to accept less than you want or deserve, just don't set your sights unreasonably high. Base your mate search on what's within your reach, not on your fantasies.

7. Lighten up

In chapter 1, we explained why meeting someone compatible is difficult. Part of the reason is, as we age, we become too set in our ways.

Tina B. Tessina, of Long Beach, Calif, an author, PhD and therapist, says: "The key for happiness in relationships after 50 is for all of us to lighten up on each other."

If you meet somebody who likes to dance, and you have two left feet and care little about dancing, do you say, "Nope, sorry, I'm unwilling to change," or do you say, "Hey, I'm not very good, but I'm willing to take lessons, and try to learn to be good enough so that at least you'll dance with me."

Lighten up and relax, and be willing to try new things. You just might enjoy a relationship with somebody who is willing to bend for you also.

Incorporate these seven tips into your dating game plan. With each little improvement, your chances of meeting someone right for you will increase.

Chapter 4

Protecting Yourself

I wish middle-age dating were as simple as getting out and having fun. Unfortunately, it's not. Many things can go wrong that can hurt you.

The purpose of this chapter is to protect you, to learn from what others have experienced. We begin with *When Meeting Strangers,* the most important section in the book. Then, we discuss four aspects of your life to protect—your heart, health, drinking glass (what's that about, you ask?) and assets. The chapter concludes with a section on red flags, which you should adopt as your dating ally.

When Meeting Strangers...

(The most important advice in this book)

If you remember nothing else, remember this short section. To meet potential mates, you need to get out with people. All kinds. You need to make new friends. You're going to come across many strangers.

Whenever meeting strangers, there is risk involved. There are people lurking out there with evil intentions who could harm you. Regardless of how you meet—on a blind date, the Internet, a personal ad, the introduction by a friend, or from being approachable or assertive, or in the produce section of the supermarket, be extraordinarily careful. Always put safety first.

If your instinct tells you something is fishy about a person, or not quite right, or too good to be true, heed your instinct and back away.

Four Cautions

- On a first or second date, meet during the day in a well-lighted place--a coffee shop or a pancake house--for example. Tell the manager you're meeting a stranger. Ask if he'll keep an eye on you

- Tell your friends with whom you're meeting, and where. Give them a contact number of your date. Some people even bring a friend along who waits in the car or remains out of sight

- Drive your own car. Don't accept a ride to your car. Be careful, a stranger can follow you, find out where you live and come back later

- Always be on your guard for danger. Avoid strangers who approach you in parking lots

Again, this is the most important section in this book.

Protect your heart

Many people our age are terribly lonely. They want more than anything to have a mate. They're vulnerable. And while loneliness can be horrible, having your heart broken at our age is worse. Be careful where you allow your heart to lead you. Listen to your brain, logic and instincts. Don't set yourself up for a broken heart. John Johnson, Washington, D.C., says: "When dating later in life, keep one foot on the ground while floating on Cloud 9."

Protect your health

Chapter 13 tackles the subject of sex. However, a warning about sex is appropriate here. My friend, Judy Fink, who works for AARP wrote, "Remind people about serious health risks from unprotected sex...HIV and AIDS are increasing in people over 50—heterosexual folks...deciding to become sexually active without testing themselves and their potential partners. I want to keep the active, enthusiastic, educated folks around longer, and this is one of the important elements in the 'plan.'"

If anybody rushes you into sex, walk away. It's too dangerous. Percentage-wise, the fastest-growing age group to contact HIV and other sexually transmitted diseases, is age 50-plus.

Protect your drink glass

Never go to a man's house on a first or second date.

--Alexis, Staten Island, NY

There's a relatively new concern middle-age daters need to be aware of as we find from Maggie Fraser's story.

Maggie ran a personal ad in a shopper magazine, a gentleman responded. Maggie says: "I was very naïve. Married 30 years. I thought everyone was a nice person. I had a date with a man. He seemed charming. We went to a small, expensive restaurant in Laguna Beach (Calif).

So far, so good. Maggie was off on the right foot with the gentlemen. A restaurant in Laguna Beach, can you imagine? (note from Tom: Laguna Beach is a very upscale, chic town). Maggie thought single life after 30 years of marriage wasn't so bad after all.

"The next week, he wanted to cook dinner for me at his home. Gee, I thought, that's a nice thing for a man to do."

Author's alert to women: When guys cook dinner for women, it impresses the heck out of them. A guy's got you in his den, and he pulls out all of the seduction weapons—wine, fresh salmon on a bed of spinach, fireplace burning (probably real logs), candles on the table, fresh roses from his garden in the bathroom (and probably on the nightstand next to his bed), Mantovani or Johnny Mathis on the CD player.

Maggie continued: "After dinner and nice conversation, I used the rest room. We then played pool in his loft. Sipping on wine—my second glass—I thought it was turning out to be a nice date. I love most games. Nice company, nice gentleman."

Sounds like a date made for lovers. A nice man is pampering and cooking for you, treating you like a queen.

"The next thing I remember it was 3 a.m. and I was in his bed. I was horrified. I just grabbed my things and ran out the front door. I had been drugged. I could have been killed. Never again did I go to a man's home. I was quite traumatized for two years. You can't imagine my fear."

So, situations to avoid: going to a man's house before you know him well enough to trust him. And, spiked drinks. If it should happen to you, report it to the authorities. Maggie didn't, "I couldn't have proven a thing," she said.
Police tell me she should have. Too bad she didn't switch wine glasses with him (and pound him with a pool cue).

In January, 2003, there was a story on AOL about a teenager who had been charged with murder for spiking another teenager's drink with cyanide, killing him. Apparently, both were in love with the same woman.

When you're out anywhere, and you're having a drink--wine, soda, coffee, fruit juice--don't let your glass or cup out of your sight.

Protect your assets

Many women over 50 are lonely, and hope they'll meet someone. They're vulnerable and can get taken financially. *The Dana Point News*--the paper for which I've written nine years--carried this news item on May 27, 1999. I inserted the xxx and deleted the man's name.

After a brief trial, Superior Court Judge John Ryan convicted Laguna Niguel resident xxx last Thursday and sentenced him to nine years in prison...A jury...deliberated for one day before convicting xxx, 61, of bilking six women out of more than $34,000.

Xxx, married 11 times, has a history spanning more than 30 years of charming women with tales of being a fireman, race car driver, contractor and pilot. After stealing women's hearts, he stole their money--draining bank accounts and borrowing money never paid back. xxxs' conviction marked the third time he has been imprisoned for defrauding women.

When I asked one of xxx's victims--who had been taken for $35,000--if she'd share her experience in a column to alert other women, she adamantly said "no," not because she was embarrassed, but, she said, "because I love him and want to help him." Remarkable what loneliness can do to logical thinking.

Senior women are particularly vulnerable. In some cases, their husbands made the financial decisions. After their husbands die, the responsibilities are on their shoulders, and they're confused.

If you start dating someone, consider hiring an investigative agency to do a background check on your new love. Get a report card on him. He won't know about it. Think of the time you'll save and the heartbreak you'll avoid if he turns out to be a bad credit risk, or, if he has a record of previous convictions. Think of the peace of mind you'll gain if he checks out okay. And think of what you'll save if he doesn't. Mature and intelligent singles are having that done.

Robyn shared her story, "I had a blind date with a friend of a girlfriend. She had known him for over tens years. Ideal good guy and family man. Huh, I was almost dragged into his bad business dealings, lies, tax liens and business debts (which are at current count of half a million). I wish I'd known beforehand." An investigation by a private investigator would have uncovered that.

Women need to be in control of their money. Be sure you protect and hang on to your money.

If a man starts talking about helping you with your finances, or suggests access to your finances in any way, that's a huge red flag. Don't fall for it. Don't loan money, thinking a promissory note will protect you.

I lent a woman I was dating $1650; she signed a promissory note. She decided to only repay $900, saying, "I was your girlfriend," as if that had value. She refused to pay the balance due, so I took her to Small Claims Court. It wasn't the money, it was the damn principle. I hired a U.S. marshal to have her served. She dodged him, refusing to open her front door on several occasions. I knew she was getting married on the bluff overlooking the Pacific Ocean at the world-famous Ritz Carlton Hotel in Dana Point, so I planned to have her served during the ceremony.

Fortunately (for both of us), I saw her a week before at the Post Office and had her served there. The court ruled against her, but she refused to pay, so I had her bank account frozen to collect. Don't go through a similar experience, simply don't lend money.

Also, before you decide to co-mingle funds with a lover, read about the pitfalls in chapter 14.

And speaking of red flags, and protecting yourself, that's the next topic.

Red Flags

People cringe when they hear the words, *red flags.* But red flags can be your dating allies, your watchdog, your radar, your early-warning system. My Webster's Dictionary defines a red flag as "a danger signal."

We've all heard the saying, "If somebody seems too good to be true, they probably are." Most of us are smart enough to notice red flags. We were born with instincts to protect ourselves. The problem is that some of us are so lonely, we choose to ignore red flags, thinking if we heed them, our opportunity to find love in a particular situation will go away (and it will, and that's good).

Friends often see red flags more clearly and objectively than we. If they're screaming, "Be careful, that new guy you met is a jerk, a con (or ex-con), a fake, a phony, or a felon," listen to them. But singles, particularly as they grow older, don't always respond wisely to friends' warnings or red flags, They let down their guard or accept a mate's bizarre behavior--they trust too much--and they end up getting burned. Here are three red flag life experiences.

A 60-year-old woman met a widower of four years through a personal ad. She said, "I fell for him big time. We were very compatible. We loved to play golf and take long walks along the beach. He wanted to move in with me," she said. But there were aspects of the man's behavior that made her suspicious.

"He wouldn't take me to his home or introduce me to his friends. He didn't want to be traceable--on my phone bill, calls to him showed as 800 000-0000. Also, while we were involved, my credit cards disappeared," she said.

"He had a hidden agenda. After a month, I insisted he show me his home or we didn't have a relationship. The man who said he loved me daily for that month just walked away. Sometimes the man of your dreams--the one you want--is a nightmare and is the last man a woman should be involved with."

It's not only women who need to heed red flags. Patrick Freeman, 59, Laguna Beach, found that out. Patrick went online to find a mate. A woman who said she lived in a nearby city responded. She was the prettiest woman to show an interest in him in a long time. In her Internet profile, she struck a sexy pose and looked to be in her late 30s or early 40s, too young for him, but worth a look.

The woman could only be reached by cell phone. During their third conversation, she said she wanted to meet, suggesting a country bar in a remote location. Patrick sensed trouble. He insisted they meet in his city.

Patrick was shocked when he saw her. She was closer to age 30. Twenty minutes into their date at the Hotel Laguna, Patrick heard a gruff voice behind him say, "What are you doing with my wife?" The man put Patrick in a head lock. Patrick lunged backward, and gave the man a sharp elbow where it hurts the most, and dialed 911 on his cell phone. In a minute, the police arrived. They arrested the man and the woman, who were known cons. Patrick suspects they were trying to blackmail him.

One woman shared a red flag story: "I attended a wedding of an older woman friend who insisted she had met the true love of her life. I have a picture of several of her friends standing together at the wedding reception. What the picture doesn't show is that all of us were saying to each other, 'This is going to be a disaster,' and it was.

"She lost her condo, self-respect and a year of her life to misery. We all tried to tell her, gently, that the man she was marrying didn't seem of good character, but she refused to listen, and because we didn't want to stop being her friends, we shut up. Make sure you introduce your prospective partner to lots of friends and family. Give them a chance to know him or her, and listen to the reactions. If one friend takes a dislike to your intended, that can be overlooked—but if you get several negative responses, pay attention! Your friends love you, and they're not blinded by 'limerence'—that delirious stage of lust/relief/hope that marks a new relationship."

The list of red flags is endless. New ones fly everyday. Here's a short list, just the tip of the iceberg.

Common Dating Red Flags

1. He can only be reached by cell phone
2. You don't know where he works or lives
3. You've never met his family or friends
4.   He's not available on week-ends
5. He's secretive. No straight answers
6. You know little about his past or present
7. He wants to meet in remote places
8. He only sits in dark booths in dark restaurants
9. He always pays by cash, never by credit card
10. You don't know if he has children
11. You catch him in a lie
12. He repeats unfavorable behavior
13. He wants to move too fast

So that's it--important advice about protecting your heart, health, drink glass and assets.

Remember: Having been out of touch for 30 years is no excuse for being naïve or gullible. Proceed wisely into the dating world. And when a red flag waves in front of your eyes, thank it for being there.

Chapter 5

Who pays? for the date

Women in southern California seem to believe it is their God-given right to look up at the ceiling or conveniently use the ladies room whenever the dinner check shows up.

--Randy Wagner, 48, Aliso Viejo, Calif.

If there's one topic that can start a war between middle-aged men and women, it's the issue of *Who pays?* for the date. When we were young, the male most always paid. But, times and rules have changed. Now, "Who pays?" is a gray area. Men believe one thing, women another.

We begin the chapter with five *Who pays?* stories. Then, we'll hear from the women, and then the men. We'll finish the chapter by establishing the definitive *Who pays?* policy once and for all.

A first (and last) date with Mr. Cheap

Becky, an 80-year-old widow living in San Juan Capistrano, Calif., was asked by a widower neighbor to join him in taking the train for lunch to Seaport Village, a bustling area in San Diego with restaurants and shops at the water's edge. Becky thought: "Oh my gosh, a real live date--the first in years."

Becky's date stepped up to the Amtrak station ticket window to purchase their tickets--at least that's what Becky thought--but, he purchased only a ticket for himself.

"I was dumbfounded," says Becky, "he didn't even consider me. He just stepped aside as if he expected me to pay for myself. Thank goodness, I had a credit card."

When the lunch check arrived, Becky's date grabbed it. Becky thought: "Now, that's better." She smiled, thinking she shouldn't have been so harsh on the guy, maybe he wasn't so bad after all.

Until he said, "Your share is $6.95."

"We didn't talk much on the train ride home," says Becky. "I knew I wouldn't date him again."

Crapped Out

A 46-year-old man paid for everything--hotel, meals, transportation--when he took a date to Las Vegas. He was on a roll at the craps table. It appeared he was going to win big money. His date stopped him, and asked him to agree to give her half of his winnings.

"I thought she was too pushy," the man said, "but I told her she could have half so we'd enjoy the rest of the weekend. I'm glad I crapped-out. She was too materialistic and broke my rhythm at the table. Don't see her anymore."

Splitting the Bill

Stan, a 52-year-old, said, "I've been dating women who make more money than I. They seem to sense this so we mainly split the cost. I had a first date with a woman; we went to the Fisherman's Restaurant on the San Clemente (Calif.) Pier. We were there most of the night. The bill was $105. I was going to pay but she insisted we split it--what a nice surprise."

Rumpelstiltskin

A few years ago, when I was dating a certain woman, I always paid. "I know you've been spending a lot of money on me lately," she said, "but I'd like to see the ballet."

"Why don't we go Dutch?" I suggested, thinking my request was reasonable, the tickets were $85 each.

She acted like Rumpelstiltskin, stomping her feet and screaming, "I've never, ever paid a penny on a date, and I don't intend to start now."

We both worked and had comparable expenses, homes and cars. There was nothing particularly wonderful about her that would warrant that I always give and she always take. I didn't understand, nor did I like, her objection to sharing.

We didn't go to the ballet. In fact, we didn't go out after that. She married a rich, older guy who doesn't seem to care that he pays for everything. If he's happy with that arrangement, the more power to him. Thank heavens he's got her now, but I don't think that makes him the winner.

Cold day in hell before she'll pay

This *Who pays?* controversy started during a speech I made at a library to 90 middle-aged singles.

When I said, "Women should be willing to ask a man out and pay for the date," a woman in the audience whispered to the woman seated next to her, "It'll be a cold day in hell before I pay for a man's dinner."

I didn't hear her comment, but a 76-year-old Ray Averett heard it. During the question-and-answer period, Ray wanted to know why the woman thought that way, and why, in the year 2003, some women are unwilling to share dating expenses.

A lively debate followed. The woman tried to explain her position, but most of the men in the room disagreed with her unwillingness to pay.

Later, Ray sent me a letter and explained his position: "The time has long passed when older single women considered the man a provider, a protector, a financial provider and someone to 'take care of them.' Unfortunately, too many older single women still think of a man that way."

Ray asked, "How do older single women relearn their priorities in dating? Perhaps many will never learn such as the woman sitting in front of me who made the comment. I live on Social Security and retirement investments and lead a conservative lifestyle, my resources aren't endless. Why should I always have to pay? I can't and won't."

The common thread of the above five stories is that confusion and opinions about *Who pays?* abound. Here's what several women said about the subject.

What women think about *Who pays?*

Column reader Jane wrote: "The man picking up the tab on a date is a tradition, and you know why—it's to impress the woman with his worthiness as a mate. Period. It's his ego acting up, not hers."

And this from Marty: "When a man expects me to pay my share of the bill, it makes me feel like less of a woman…the whole bill, it makes me feel like a fool."

One woman requesting not to be identified wrote: "I take issue with women paying for dates…men should pay for dates. I feel I am taking the male role if I pay. It makes me uncomfortable, as if I'm not respected."

Joyce, Philadelphia, added: "In a purely dating situation, I'm from the 'old school' where the 'boy' pays."

Nanci, from Orange County, blamed discussing this topic on me: "Just because you don't want to pay the cost of dating, you are trying to make everyone believe that that is the way it is now. There are still gentlemen out there who pay for dinners."

And this from Linda, "If I were to date a man for a while and I believed he really cared about me and treated me the way I want to be treated, I would at some point offer to buy him dinner. During the courting phase, men should always pay."

"Definitely the man should pay--chivalry isn't dead-- unless the woman invited him," says Libby, a 50-ish woman who recently remarried.

Mae has a practical and realistic outlook on who pays, "If I suggest a special place or something I want to do, I treat. If I prepare dinner, and then we go dancing, the dancing's his treat. If a friend takes me to dinner and dancing because he doesn't want to go alone, I never offer to pay in a situation like that. Who pays depends on a man's financial situation, his ego and how he feels about paying."

Jean prefers to pay for herself or share 50-50. "Then, I don't feel obligated, it's enjoying the person, not whether he can pay for an expensive dinner. A walk on the beach or game of cards can be as fun."

Nancy summed up the "Who pays?" issue quite nicely: "I'm not a feminist, but I do feel comfortable paying my way on a date. I've found that it equalizes the relationship and removes the expectation of a reward (sex) or entitlement (free meal). When one person pays for the other's entertainment regularly, the balance of power in the relationship is unequal and immature."

Amy Alkon (www.advicegoddess.com), a syndicated columnist, wrote a column in *The Orange County Register,* titled, "Courting costs are yours, too, ladies." Amy wrote: "If a woman considers herself a man's equal, her equality shouldn't evaporate when the check comes. The point here isn't calculating each person's outlay to the bent dime. Just that dating shouldn't send men to the bankruptcy court and women to the mall."

What men think about *Who pays?*

"Sometimes, I feel like a walking wallet," says Bob Pace, 44, Irvine, Calif., "I enjoy being chivalrous, but it's nice when a woman offers to pay. Today, women sometimes make as much as the men."

Bob said, "I was in a nice growing relationship with a woman. It was warm, affectionate, close, with good communication, many common interests and a good level of trust. I felt there might be a future in it. Then one day, she told me she was ending the relationship because I wasn't able to spend money on her as generously as she would like. I was hurt…interesting a woman would trash a good relationship for money."

"I don't have a problem with my date picking up the whole dinner tab on alternate dates," added Fred of Dallas.

Joe F, 51, Los Angeles, finds the *Who pays?* controversy very much alive there. He said, "…She hasn't offered to help pay for anything on any dates…so I guess I have met another one of those 'freeloader women,' that I seem to find everywhere. She works, has a nice house, so what's the deal?

"I drive a ten-year-old Honda, live in a one-bedroom apartment, and work for a non-profit agency...is there something about my 'resume' that says this is a wealthy guy?"

Ray Averett shared this story. "On a cruise, I met a charming single woman in one of the lounges. We enjoyed talking and dancing so much that we agreed to meet again the next night. We met eleven straight nights. I paid for the drinks, and not once did she offer to pay. After the eleventh night, I asked her why she hadn't offered and she said, 'Why should I? I've been providing you with my company. Haven't you been enjoying that?.'

"I said, 'I have been providing you with my company also.' I avoided her the rest of the cruise. That was her loss as well as mine."

The final word on *Who pays?*

Based on the information presented in this chapter, and the inputs of column readers over the last nine years, a middle-ground list of *Who pays?* guidelines that men and women can hopefully live with follows on the next page.

Who pays? guidelines

- In Chapter 3, we said it's important for women to become more assertive in dating. You may be asking men on dates--for coffee, dinner, a movie, or the theatre. When you do, assume that you'll be paying

- On the first date, the person who did the asking—man or woman—pays

- If the man asks the woman out, he pays for the first few dates. But, she should offer at least a small gesture, like treating for ice cream or a movie, or cooking him dinner

- If a couple starts to date on a regular basis, they need to discuss the finances and adopt an expense-sharing plan that works best for them. Mary Lotz, age 57, Irvine, Calif., writes, "My sweetheart pays for all the dining out and entertainment, I compensate by cooking, doing picnic lunches, deserts, etc. He's happy." Where affordability is an issue, a woman can be creative as Mary describes. Men appreciate that. And no one keeps score

- There are no hard and fast *Who pays?* rules. But, if a woman never or seldom offers, men will notice. Relationships are about sharing. If a woman is mired in the "I want it the old-fashioned way" mentality, and is unwilling to take a more active role in the financing of courtship, she may notice her phone is ringing less for dates, or not at all

- Guys appreciate when women share expenses, and most won't enter relationships with women unwilling to do so. Neither men nor women should always have to be the banker in a relationship. Women's roles have changed--in the workplace, at home and in dating

- The old arguments--affordability, tradition, because we're gentlemen, the male role, during the courting phase, the way it's always been and the way I was raised, are no longer valid. It's the 21st century, times and circumstances have changed. Middle-age relationships are about equality and sharing

- Some men don't agree that it's OK for women to pay. When a woman picks up the tab, men should accept graciously. Doing otherwise could be a put-down to her. If men are so unenlightened they won't let a woman pay, they deserve to have their pockets emptied

- Under no circumstances should a woman feel "sexually obligated" when a man pays. You're on a date, not at a swap meet. If a man expects sex, a hug, a kiss, or a squeeze-- because he paid for the date--he's wrong and totally out of place

- Greta Cohn, of San Clemente, Calif., a school teacher in her 50s, sums up the *Who pays?* question beautifully, "Sharing expenses or taking turns paying is part of a successful philosophy I have adopted in my later life. Deepak Chopra says, 'Every relationship is give and take. Giving engenders receiving and receiving engenders giving.' That's a great way to live."

So, for once and for all, the final answer to the *Who pays?* question is: **It depends on the circumstances.**

Chapter 6

Identify the qualities you want in a mate

My marriages to drunks caused the breakups.

--A divorced woman vowing not to repeat her mistakes

When middle-aged people decide to date, they should make a list of the personal qualities they seek in a mate.

Having a list is important

Most of us need to improve our choice of mates. Many of us end up with the same type of person we failed with before. Or, we select a mate who isn't right for us. This is evident by the divorce rates of second and third marriages, which exceed 70 percent.

Many of us approach meeting someone as a hit or miss chance. Someone comes along we're attracted to and we fall for them, regardless of compatibility. We need to be mature enough to know the type of person who is right for us.

"I won't become involved with a man unless he has a job, a car and a home," said a Dana Point, Calif., realtor. She's wise, she knows what she wants in a mate, and dating a man who is financially secure is important to her. Why should she be the bank for a man?

Many who re-enter the dating scene don't think about what they want in a mate. Perhaps they were married 30 years or more, and have no idea of the type of person who would be right for them.

Often they become involved with a person (not right for them) with unfavorable results. Down the road, another failed relationship: wasted emotions, energy, money and time. As we age, failing again is a heavy burden. Most of us hope our next relationship will be our last. By improving our selection of a mate, we increase our chances of that happening.

What a list won't do

A list won't make finding a mate easier. You'll still have to venture out into the dating world and play the numbers game. But a list will help you decide whether or not to continue dating a person you've met.

Nor will a list guarantee relationship success. Lori, a widow, said, "It's foolish for middle-aged people not to know what they want in a relationship. I have a list. I met a man with every qualification on it--except I forgot to write that he shouldn't be married. He hasn't lived with his wife in nine years, but his children will never accept anyone new in his life."

Another reader asked, "Doesn't having a list make dating too scripted? Whatever happened to good old-fashioned falling in love?"

For people our age, relying only on old-fashioned falling in love can have disastrous results. Important qualities might be overlooked. A list will help you make a better decision.

Why people make lists

After three failed marriages and a shattered relationship, I made a list. Chemistry and looks had always been important to me. I tended to be with younger women.

I thought about what I was doing wrong (too much emphasis on chemistry and looks) and put together a list of qualities I wanted in a mate. It took me 58 years to approach dating maturely. Months later, I met a woman with the characteristics I had written down. We've been together for five years. We're compatible; that's critical.

Linda Binley, of Laguna Niguel, Calif., made a list after burning out on the dating scene. "Putting my desires in writing clarified what I wanted. I didn't review my list until my husband and I had been together for two years. When I did, I rated him an 85 percent. The list helped solidify my thinking," she said.

Keith Stroud, 65, a retired school principal and author, feels having a list is critical. "I've been divorced twice and can't afford another marriage mistake," says Keith. "If I had maintained a list during my last marriage, I would have realized that she was the woman of my dreams, and I would have changed my behavior and treated her better. Maybe we'd still be married."

Put your list in writing

Keep it simple, ten items or so, ranked in the order of importance. Prioritize each quality by putting a point total alongside, with a maximum of 10 points. For example, if the most important characteristic is having your mate make

49

you the top priority, assign 10 points. Next, if you want someone who cares about his health, and is financially secure, but these qualities aren't quite as important, assign lesser points. The total points on your list don't matter. You're merely putting numbers alongside to rank the importance of each item. For example:

1. **Makes me his top priority** **(10)**

2. **Cares about his health** **(9)**

3. **Is financially secure** **(8)**

The two cardinal rules of list making

First: What we seek in a mate, we must give in return. Relationships are about fairness and sharing. No double standards allowed. You can't expect kindness from your mate, and not be kind in return. You can't expect to be treated as number one, if you don't treat him as number one. Relationships need to be well-balanced.

Second: Never pull out your list during a date (unless you're a turkey, or you want it to end immediately).

Be flexible. A list is only a guide

Review and adjust your list occasionally. Add an item, drop another, or change the priority.

Don't be so inflexible that if someone comes along who doesn't have all of the qualities on your list, you dismiss him. Perhaps, he has qualities you can adjust to, and vice versa. A list is only a tool to help you choose the right type of person.

Alexis says, "A mate has to be someone with at least 85 percent of the qualities I want because even 15 percent of the qualities I DON'T WANT is not a good thing." At least Alexis is willing to bend some.

And William F. Buckley, of Gulf Shores, Ala., warns, "You better be ready to use some 'variables' in your criteria, or you're not going to find anyone. Compromise is the key and the ability to adapt is essential. This does not mean that one should lower one's standards, just that the ability to accept change and the ability to adapt are necessary."

Added benefit: comparing the loves in your life

By adding columns to your list, you can make it a tool to compare relationships—and gain some insight into why some worked and others failed.

Add three or four columns to your list. Write the name of your ex or ex's above the first columns and the name of your new love above the right-hand column.

For each person, assign points to each quality. This is a subjective judgment. Then, simply multiply the priority-number by the number of points you assigned. You'll get a weighted average, which measures both the importance of the quality and how your ex-partners stack up in each quality. See the next page for a simple, short example.

Comparing your ex to a new person

	ex-Jack	**ex-Joe**	**new-Bill**
1. I'm his top priority (10)	6 (60)	4 (40)	7 (70)
2. Cares about health (9)	4 (36)	3 (27)	8 (72)
3. Is financially secure (8)	3 (24)	3 (24)	2 (16)
Total Points	120	91	158

In this simple example, Bill--the new guy--looks good after the first three items. The biggest drawback, he's not financially secure, and since that matters to you (you assigned a point value of 9), that might be a red flag. Also note, in this example, all of the mates scored low in category 3—financially secure. This could mean you're meeting men in the wrong places.

Finish evaluating each quality, and then total the points. You'll get a bird's-eye view of who's potentially better for you, who isn't and who wasn't. You may unravel the mystery of why a relationship worked and others failed. Don't make a marriage decision based on this exercise, it's merely a tool to help you make better selections.

A sample Qualities-Wanted Comparison List is on the next page.

Qualities-Wanted Comparison List

	Ex # One	Ex # Two	New
1. I'm his top priority (10)	(___)___	(___)___	(___)___
2. Feel Natural (10)	(___)___	(___)___	(___)___
3. Positive Attitude (10)	(___)___	(___)___	(___)___
4. Carefree; Relaxed (8)	(___)___	(___)___	(___)___
5. Respects Me (8)	(___)___	(___)___	(___)___
6. Gives me space (7)	(___)___	(___)___	(___)___
7. Chemistry, warmth (7)	(___)___	(___)___	(___)___
8. Sense of Humor (6)	(___)___	(___)___	(___)___
9. Finances okay (6)	(___)___	(___)___	(___)___
10. Spontaneous (5)	(___)___	(___)___	(___)___

TOTAL POINTS: _____   _____   _____

Chapter 7

Tread Lightly With These 4 Situations

A therapist told me the average time to get over a divorce is 5 to 7 years. I tend to date very, very casually someone who is newly separated or divorced, for that reason. Way too much baggage.

--Robin Nugent, Buena Park, Calif.

1. Rebound Relationships

Can rebound relationships work? Most singles will experience a rebound relationship. Either they'll be on the rebound, or they'll meet a person who is.

Let's assume your relationship of x years ends. Regardless of who ended it, your heart is drained and empty. You take a dating sabbatical. You're hurt and need time alone to heal.

Then, too soon, when you're not looking, not dating, not mentally available (you flunked the *Mental Preparedness* test in Chapter 2), a quality person crosses your path. He's a cut above the rest. He has many of the items on your qualities-wanted list. If the timing were different, you know you could love him and be happy. He wants to date you. Your head says yes; your heart isn't ready.

You don't have the capacity to give enough to make the relationship work, at least not now. Trying wouldn't be fair to him. But, you also know at your age, quality people don't come along very often. There may never be another of his character to cross your path. What do you do?

First, be honest with yourself. Determine if your interest in the new man is because you're lonely, and see him as a replacement to ease the hurt, or, because you see a potential relationship in the future. If he's just a filler, don't get involved.

After a few casual dates, he wants a relationship. If he's as special as you think, he'll be willing to discuss your dilemma. He may or may not realize or accept that your heart is broken and will take time to heal.

If he understands and is willing to wait and take the risk that you might never love him--or you might go back to your ex--it's okay to proceed cautiously. Be sure he knows it might take months or a couple of years for your head to clear and your heart to grow healthy. Don't set a timetable. Rebound relationships require mature people.

If, along the way, he tries to rush you or feels you're progressing too slowly, or starts being demanding, you'll have to bow out.

As time goes by, your ex may still be on your mind, avoid talking about him to your new friend. After all, the new guy is being patient with you, don't beat him over the head about it, or ever use it as a weapon in an argument.

If you find your heart isn't healing, and the new guy is more of a friend--and that's all he'll ever be--step to the line and be unselfish enough to tell him. If that's the case, let him go, so he can find a life with someone else, and perhaps you can too.

If your original instincts about him were correct, somewhere in the future you may have a far superior relationship with him than you had with your ex. A new relationship built on honesty, patience, and respect may be a much stronger relationship than before.

2. Long-Distance Relationships

After nine years of writing newspaper columns, it amazes me how many middle-age singles are involved in long-distance relationships. The Internet is the primary reason because it's easy to meet people online from all over the country and the world.

Monica Jones considers herself to be the "queen of long-distance relationships." A few years ago, when Monica lived in Mission Viejo, Calif., she worked for a website company approving personal ads. In one of the ads, she liked the way a Florida man named Greg looked and what he had written in his profile. She e-mailed Greg, they chatted online and then by telephone. A month later, the 33-year-old divorcee went to Florida to meet him.

Monica shared sound advice for people considering relocating to be near a new lover.

Monica Jones's Tips

1. Meet in person within a month so you won't invest a lot of time, money and emotions into someone who may not be what you're looking for. If you aren't physically attracted, you won't want a relationship. Face-to-face chemistry is unpredictable (see chapter 11, Internet Dating) on this important point

2. When you first meet, have a back-up plan—to stay at a hotel or return home sooner if the visit doesn't go as planned

3. Spend several weeks with the person at different times of the year before moving

4. Meet and spend quality time with his family, friends and children

5. Don't be in a long-distance relationship with someone you can't trust. Wondering if what he's telling you is true will drive you nuts

6. Try not to go weeks or months without spending time together. People can change in that amount of time, and you may not be able to recognize the change via the phone or computer

7. Have different methods of contacting each other--the person's home, work, cell, and pager numbers, and e-mail address. He should be willing to give those to you

8. If you decide to move, discuss expectations beforehand. If it doesn't work, both will have an exit plan. This is like a marriage pre-nuptial agreement, instead it covers moving to be together

9. Have at least one back-up plan if the move doesn't work out. Make sure you can return to your old life if you need to. Don't join assets until you are in a committed relationship, whether it's marriage or another arrangement (before co-mingling funds, read chapter 14)

Did Monica's relationship work? A year after meeting Greg, she moved to Florida. A year and a half later, they were married. A year after that, Monica gave birth to a boy.

Most long-distance relationships don't work, and few work out as well as Monica's and Greg's. But if people follow Monica's advice, and move slowly, and are honest with each other, they can have a beautiful life together by overcoming the miles between them.

A long-distance relationship that didn't work

The Internet makes it possible for a single person living in a city where there aren't many available singles to meet someone in an area where there are. Such was the case with Mary of Modesto, Calif. With little dating action there, she used the Internet to meet Ben, who lived 300 miles away in Orange County.

Mary said, "We wrote back and forth a lot, talked on the phone and he came up to see me. He paid for me to fly down several times to spend extended week-ends with him. He introduced me to his grown children, you sort of feel safe when they do that. He discussed in front of them me coming to live with him."

Mary moved to Orange County. "I gave up my job of three years, my two beautiful cats (he had a parrot and wouldn't allow them), an apartment and a lot of friends," said Mary. "His daughter adopted my cats so I could be comfortable with where the cats were living. Fortunately, I got a job right away."

So far so good. Two singles meet over the Internet. They take time getting to know each other. Trust is established. They want to build a life together so one of them moves.

Mary continued: "I think he felt secure with my being gone, working all day, and he was semi-retired, so he ventured back on the Internet and hooked up with another lady for the daytime hours. I found out because she left seductive voice mails in the middle of the night after he was asleep and I heard them. He said…'oh that is a poor lady who is fat, no self-esteem, and I'm just helping her.'" Who can blame Mary for being leery?

"While he was out with her, I had access to his computer. Seems the e-mails were a carbon copy of what he sent me with the name changed," said Mary, "When he found out I had checked his computer, he stormed into my office and told me my stuff was out on the steps of his home and to never come back." He didn't allow Mary to gather her necessities; she was locked out, in a big city, knowing no one, two weeks after moving in with him, and terrified.

"It took nine months to rebuild my life, get my own apartment and finally become reunited with all my belongings. He had my jewelry and all the things I had in my safe deposit box in his house," said Mary.

Mary says she learned a valuable lesson: "Don't trust what someone says online. If they're so good, why are they looking out of their area for someone? I saw no red flags because it seemed so normal. If my story helps just one woman to not jeopardize her job, home or financial security, I'll be happy."

"He asked me to come down here and move in with him. I think I'm a very intelligent woman, but in matters of love, we become ignorant because we WANT to believe someone loves us."

Mary added, "If he had been truthful and suggested I get my own apartment, that would have been more upfront. We could have dated and if it didn't work out, then fine."

Before uprooting your life, evaluate the possible consequences. Being alone and lonely is one thing, but making a decision to be with someone and having it backfire is far worse.

What readers say

- Eileen Ganong, San Clemente, "Women must learn to put together a life that is rich and fulfilling, with or without a man. If we have a life that we enjoy, it will be harder to give that up for a virtual stranger. In the story above, Mary's friend Ben didn't give up anything. That was the first red flag. Mary should have rented an apartment, we should never hand over responsibility for those choices to somebody else. Mary could have made the decision to get her own place. We shouldn't expect someone else to look out for our best interests."

- Giselle Blum, New Orleans: "Short visits or trips together are no substitute for staying a week in the home of the new lover. During that time, forego the fancy dinners and parties and do day-to-day stuff. If the man works, he shouldn't take time off. This will enable the couple to see if they can cope with daily life together.

- Mary Martin, San Clemente, "Long-distance relationships cloud reality. You spend so little time together you're willing to overlook a lot. It works until you make it permanent. Then, the things that were hinted at previously manifest. Often in life, when opportunity presents itself, reason escapes us. I would not look for a long-distance relationship, but when the love bug bites, sane decisions cease!"

3. Dating at work

The hardest part is that I work with him and the day after we broke up.....my job got changed and my desk is now in his space.

--a woman on the pitfalls of dating at work

As singles grow older, finding people to date becomes progressively more difficult. Singles need to be creative in searching for places to meet other singles. There are many stories of people who met at work, fell in love, and went on to have successful relationships. Dating at work can and does happen because it's easy to meet someone there. You get to know people well by working alongside and observing them interacting with others, and seeing them under stress. Some of these relationships work, it's just the consequences of failure that are so unpleasant. The downside is greater than the upside. Before dating a fellow employee, consider these factors.

Dating at work considerations

- If you date a co-worker on a regular basis, how do you keep it private? Somebody is bound to see you together, and then the entire office will know. You'll be under a microscope; rumors will fly

- An office romance can be wonderful--you see each other every day—as long as it works. But, what happens when things sour? When you see the person in the hall, the cafeteria, or at a meeting, it'll be awkward. You'll curse yourself (and probably him) for having been involved

- When couples fall in love at work, often company policy will force one of them to leave. In that case, someone's career goes on the back burner. Then, if it doesn't work, that person is out of a relationship and a job

- Some companies, including the military, forbid their workers from dating fellow employees. The risk of collusion and security compromise is too high

- Most bars and restaurants won't hire couples. Cocktail servers and bartenders working together can easily rip-off a place. And if the couple fights, it makes everyone around them uncomfortable.

"It's Just Lunch," a Los Angeles dating service, conducted a survey and found that 94 percent of men and 81 percent of women said they don't date co-workers. But almost 40 percent of each gender admitted they had. I guess most of them found out it was a bad idea. Dating someone at work can be tempting, but it's best to look beyond the workplace.

In her book, "The Unofficial Guide to Dating Again,' Tina Tessina writes, "I recommend replicating those positive parts of office romance somewhere else. For example, in a non-profit group, a church, a recreational group, a political campaign. If you get involved in these pursuits, you can get all the advantages of taking your time, observing the other people, etc. In a voluntary activity, the consequences are minor, the rewards are great."

4. Dating when health is an issue

Keith Stroud looks 55, exercises, doesn't drink or smoke, and takes good care of himself. He dated a woman four times. She seemed like an ideal match until he mentioned he'd had a quadruple-bypass. She quickly dumped him.

One of the important considerations in middle age relationships is health. Let's say you're dating someone and find out he or she has a health problem. Or you have a health problem. Should health matter?

"When you find a wonderful partner, every moment is precious. Celebrate life!" said Pearl Hedlund, "Many people have lived over twenty-plus years after a bypass—what guarantee do we have that any of us will live past today?"

Audri Hume, Laguna Hills, Calif., dated a man 15-years-older, who wore hearing aids, and had arthritis. "I'm sure he stopped e-mailing me because he feels too old and incapacitated. It wouldn't have bothered me. I was happy to be with such good company," Audri wrote.

"If a person has come out of the long-term care of a seriously ill spouse, parent, or child, that person has a legitimate concern about doing that again. However, if a guy is a great person, and I have a close relationship with him, I wouldn't worry about the health issue," says Jan Phillips, Tustin, Calif.

What if you're the one with the health problem? Should you reveal it to a person you've just started to date? If so, how soon?

Most singles agree that honesty and early disclosure are important. Gale Dundrea, Leicester, North Carolina, said, "If the relationship becomes serious, he'd find out sooner or later anyway. Then what? He'd feel that he'd been deceived and trust then becomes a problem. Before my 19th surgery, men would back off just knowing I needed another operation. The ironic thing is I've got all my original parts. My son said the right man wouldn't back off, and then, the right man appeared in my life at the ripe young age of 65 (he's 67). His name is Ian Kilmer and his birthday is the same day as mine. We were born within two hours of each other's birth times. We'll be married soon."

One reason to disclose your health problems early is to protect yourself. Why fall in love and then suffer the heartbreak of losing your lover when she or he finds out about your problem, and leaves?

And what happens if the partner you've been with—perhaps for years—gets sick? Do you stick it out?

Most people—not all—stay. Some take the cowardly way out. Luenne, of Hitchcock, Texas, said, "When I got in this wheelchair 14 years ago, at age 45, my hubby left for a walking woman."

That's not the case with Dave and Norma Bowe, of Laguna Niguel, Calif., married 41 years. When Norma became confined to a wheel chair, Dave purchased her a white van with special hand controls, so she can drive on her own. "I've regained my freedom," Norma said. Dave is as proud as Norma is happy. "My parents have shown the meaning of 'in sickness and in health,' and 'for better or worse,' daughter Tracy said.

Health issues should be dealt with in the same manner as other dating issues. If people are honest, caring, considerate, and understand what's important in life, they will overcome obstacles and enjoy a rewarding relationship.

Should a person's health be on your list of qualities wanted? Only you can judge that. If you meet someone and you're aware he or she is sick, you need to ask yourself, "Am I willing to standby him if he gets worse?" If the answer is no, don't get involved.

If you are faced with any of the above situations— rebound or long distance relationships, dating at work, or where health is a consideration, evaluate each carefully. Don't let loneliness make a decision for you. Before making significant life changes, determine the consequences.

Chapter 8

Older Dating Younger

"Older men want considerably younger women so they can prove to the world that everything still works.

--Harriet Kader, Huntington Beach, Calif.

In my nine years of writing about relationships, no subject is more controversial than older dating younger. And it's not just older men dating younger women that stirs the pot. When older women date younger men, eyebrows are raised. It seems everybody has an opinion on the topic.

Older men dating younger women

What women say

My friend Anne is 60. She said, "Some men 60-plus are looking on the Internet for lady matches from ages 40 to 60. There's no way an older woman—no matter how good she looks--can compete with a 40-year-old, so why even bother to respond?"

Chris Ruth, of East Anaheim, Calif., says, "I'm a 49-year-old-divorcee and find men my age looking for younger women. I won't consider a man who's looking in the 35-50 age range. It's obvious he won't be happy with a woman my age if he thinks he can 'get' a 35-year-old."

Nancy A., who lives in the Antelope Valley north of Los Angeles, says, "If you're a woman over 50 or 60, it's hard to find a man at that age who isn't looking for a younger woman. After he finds out that he can't keep up with the younger woman, he'll search for someone his own age he can feel comfortable with."

Barbara Gilvary, Laguna Hills, Calif., says, "Younger women aren't looking for older men, only what's in their back pockets. They tolerate the men's ages if there's enough money. Older men aren't interested in younger women if the beauty isn't there."

What the younger women say

It's only right to let women who are dating comment on why they're with older men. Two women shared their views.

Beth said, "I'm 29, my boyfriend is 43. I'm with him for what he does for me physically and mentally. I don't want his money and would be too proud to take it. Some of us younger chicks don't give a damn about material things. We want trust, companionship and safe sex without hassling with immature boys our own age"

Dorrie Steele, 50, Mission Viejo, Calif., said, "I always thought when I met my ideal mate, he would be around my age. So when I met Elliott Ryal (also quoted in this book), I tried to set him up with older female friends. As I grew to know Elliott, I realized he possessed all the traits I was looking for in a relationship except he was 15 years older. I decided to keep him for myself. Now, I'm a firm believer, you get what you ask for. It just may come to you in a different package. And what about the age difference? I'm having trouble keeping up with him!

What men say

Reader Bill wrote: "I'm a 50-year-old divorced male and just met a 35-year-old woman who has never married. She convinced me that I'm the greatest. I feel the relationship has a limited lifespan. What do you think? Happy but puzzled."

Limited lifespan? It depends on how soon Bill shows her his balance sheet and paycheck stub. If they're big enough, she might hang out with him for awhile. If the money runs out, she won't be far behind.

Patrick Freeman says, "Younger women are less serious and intense. They like having fun and are spontaneous. Yet, when younger women have kids at home, we older guys get bumped far down the priority list." The last time I saw Patrick he was settled in with a woman about his age, and happier than I've ever seen him.

Older women dating younger men

Women fifty-plus ask: "Where are the men our age?" Who can blame them for looking to other age groups for companionship? I've heard women say younger men treat them with more respect than the older guys. Several women who date younger men shared their thoughts, experiences, and reasons why.

Leslie said, "Dating younger men has lots of advantages. They are full of energy and optimism, and have a zest for life. They exercise and have great bodies.

Money never seems to be the problem with younger men. I take dating seriously, and have yet to have a bad date."

Connie Presley-Atchley, Trabuco Canyon, Calif., says, "I'm married to Pete, 20 years younger than I. We have a wonderful relationship and a passion for each other. I wouldn't consider a man who didn't love the same 'loves' that I do. I have a passion for horses and dogs, as does Pete. We just celebrated our 10th year together—it still is as exciting today as it was 10 years ago."

A 61-year-old woman said: "Guys my age don't e-mail back because they want someone younger. So do I. Only the young ones can keep up with me. I e-mailed a fellow who made a typo error and he turned out to be my son's age, and when I told him, he said, 'I have a mother your age, and it doesn't bother me.' At least he can stay up past 10 p.m. and likes to do things besides watch TV.

"I say go for it ladies and who cares what other people think? It's your life. Also, older men worry about their money and anyone invading their space."

Karen Robinson, Rancho Santa Margarita, Calif., said: "I've dated younger men, and find it refreshing. They're more exciting and spontaneous than older men, which I like. Older men can be too regimented. Why is an older woman ridiculed by society for dating a younger man?"

"I find men my age or a little older not a good match. Older women with younger men depends on the particular man, and the health and energy level of the woman," says Kay Van Gunst, Laguna Woods, Calif.

Ivory Dorsey, 54, Mableton, Georgia, says, "The physical attributes young men bring to the relationship don't make up for the deficit in sheer maturity and knowledge that only comes through living. Younger men deserve to explore all of the 'doing' that comes with youth, and I deserve to explore all of the 'being' that comes with maturity. It doesn't FIT."

And a South Carolina woman wrote: "I had a relationship with a man 17 years my junior, but knew from the beginning that it was just for fun and there was no way we'd ever last long-term. After the physical attraction wore off, there was nothing that we had in common except music."

An anonymous woman added, "Older women are easy to talk to, more understanding, established financially, know how to cook and entertain and have no young children around."

The feeling seems to be that older women enjoy the "fling" aspect of dating younger guys for the short-term. But, they hedge about the long-term, with concerns mainly about the difference in life's experiences, goals, and maturity levels.

So, what's best?

The points below apply to both sexes dating younger counterparts.

- Couples with an age gap can work well. It's how closely they think together, whether they enjoy being together and how compatible they are that matters. Enjoy life. Don't worry about the age difference or what others say

- If older people think, feel and act young, they may be better suited for someone younger. They wouldn't be happy with someone closer to their age who thinks old

- Some, not all, older men who date younger women are kidding themselves. They think the younger women love them, but the reality is that the younger women are usually with them for their money, power, or assets. The same applies to older women dating younger men. A woman needs to ask, why is this young stud hanging out with me? Is it for love or does he want to get his hands on my assets? In these scenarios, it sounds like the sexes are using each other. Beauty and youth for money and age. Sort of a what's-in-it-for-me, what's-in-it-for-you mentality. If people are happy with such an arrangement, that's all that matters

- It's human nature to hope for an attractive mate, most men and women begin by looking for someone younger. Many of them are missing an opportunity by not considering someone older. If more people considered dating someone older, there would be fewer lonely people

- Most people match up better with mates close to their age. They share the songs, dances and historical events they experienced and have similar energy levels.

  Anybody care to dance the Stroll or the Funky Chicken?

Chapter 9

Two Situations To Avoid

Middle-aged dating is filled with opportunities to make mistakes. This book tries to steer you clear of them. There are two situations in particular you need to avoid, which we discuss in this chapter.

Don't expect someone else to improve your life

A tremendous sense of self is required to love another person. Most of us don't have it. We're looking for another person to supply us with a sense of our own worth.

--Bobbi Atkins, Mission Viejo, Calif.

For some, life hasn't turned out as they had hoped. Perhaps they're alone and lonely, or don't have enough money, or don't own a home, or they can't afford a new car, or they don't have health insurance—the list could go on and on. They think they might meet somebody who in their eyes, is better off than they are, and by hooking up with that person, their life will get better.

They communicate with someone who sounds perfect for them. And they believe the new person is their salvation. Some make desperate, quick and foolish decisions, hoping to improve their lives. They think moving to be with the other person will make things better for them--they won't be lonely anymore, or worry about finances, or this or that. The Internet often plays a part in this scenario by connecting people who live in different parts of the country.

The Philadelphia-California connection

A 44-year-old Pennsylvania man met a 32-year-old California woman online. Each had two children. They exchanged photographs, hundreds of e-mails, and found they had so much in common, they decided to marry and merge their families. She planned to move. He sent her roses and cards while she made him underwear with hearts sewn into the crotch.

They thought meeting in person before marrying would be wise (Who said singles aren't intelligent?)

He flew to Los Angeles to see her. She planned a romantic week-end by booking three nights in a fancy beachfront hotel with an in-room spa. She didn't sleep much before he arrived. You can imagine her anxiety while she waited at the gate at LAX (this was before 9/11, when people were allowed to wait at the gate). The man she had agreed to marry was almost in her arms. The wait had been so long, so worth it. She vowed to be a good wife.

After the passengers had left the gate area, each feared the other hadn't shown because they hadn't seen each other. The two of them were all that remained. They hadn't recognized each other because both had sent photos taken years before, and both had gained a considerable amount of weight.

She noticed he had shaved, but missed a few spots. He was wearing a wrinkled tank top, old tennis shoes and blue polyester bell bottoms with holes in the knees. His hair stuck out on both sides like Bozo the clown's. He was five-nine, 250 pounds. A beeper was attached to his fly (after all, he had to carry it *somewhere*). She couldn't kiss him. Her love turned to dust. Relationship over before baggage claim. The months had been wasted on fantasy. Both had thought someone else would improve their lives. He spent the week-end in Los Angeles alone.

The Florida-California Connection

In another case, a California woman met a Florida man over the telephone during a yacht-sale transaction. After several conversations, he asked if she was single. Yes she was. They discovered they had both grown up in Indiana-- he in Indianapolis, she in nearby Kokomo. They had graduated from high school the same year. They practiced the same religion. They had so much in common (loved Indiana high school basketball), they felt meeting was fate.

She allowed him to visit at Thanksgiving and arranged for him to sleep on a yacht in a nearby harbor. They didn't share the same bed. On the fourth night, he proposed and asked her to move to Florida to live with him and to get married on Valentine's Day (in just over two months). She gave up her apartment, furniture, job, family heirlooms and car, and left in December. "He's the most romantic man I've ever met," she told me the day before she left. I was happy for her because I knew she'd recently had bad luck with men. At the Tampa Airport, he pasted white paper roses on the concrete for her from the car to the gate.

In mid-January, she walked into my deli. I looked around to see if yacht-broker Bill was with her, figuring they had returned to tie up loose ends before getting married. I was surprised to see her because she hadn't left any loose ends when she went to Florida. She looked at me sadly, shrugged her shoulders, and said, "I didn't know him well enough when I moved." (Imagine that, after being together for four days). She was in tears; I felt bad for her. She said they weren't compatible, explaining, for example, that the two biggest days in Bill's life were Elvis Presley's birthday, and the day race car driver Dale Earnhardt died.

She had to start over; the move set her back financially at least two years. She was also an emotional wreck.

The Long Island (NY)–Chicago connection

A married, Long Island, NY, woman e-mailed "I've met the most marvelous, fantastic, exciting, sexy, intelligent man and we are deeply in love."

"Where did you meet?" I asked.

"In an Internet chat room."

"What's he like in person?"

They hadn't met in person, and yet she was ready to pack up her two kids and move to Chicago to be with him. He was also married, but neither marriage--hers nor his-- was an obstacle. When I suggested she should think this over--she hadn't even seen the man in person--she replied: "I never seen God either but love Him above all." At that point, I let the conversation drop, I couldn't help her.

The Washington D.C.-California connection

A woman from Washington, D.C., e-mailed: "A recently divorced friend claims he's met his 'love' over the Internet. After writing and calling for months, she arrived here last Wednesday. They're going back to Calif., selling her condo, and returning to buy a house, where he and his two girls can live. He's known her all of four days. Is this crazy?"

A San Francisco man shared his Internet experience: "After living alone in the same residence for 21 years, I fell for a charming, vivacious woman living in Georgia. I succumbed to my loneliness, married her in late 2000, and moved to Georgia.

"Things didn't work out. I'm back, starting over, ruined financially, driving an old $300 car and trying to put my life back together."

A Jackson High School (Mich.) classmate, who still lives in the Midwest, e-mailed this story: "Out of the blue, a friend asked his wife for a divorce...getting together with a woman out east he'd 'met' on the Internet (not sure whether he had met her in person at that point)...they married. Some months later, he asked his first wife if they could get back together...of course, she said 'no'...he moved back here anyway...his two married daughters would hardly speak to him...then he tried to get back together with the second woman who said no. Wow, how to screw up your life!"

One California woman who sold her house and moved to Chicago to be with a man, said, "I'm still paying the price--emotionally and financially. Emotionally, not over the guy any longer, but what I gave up financially and how difficult it is to get my life back. I was foolish to sell my home. When I returned, I didn't have a job or furniture."

These people didn't fall in love. They fell in love with the idea of love and made life-changing decisions that put themselves in a deeper hole than before. They thought by having an, "Oh, what-the-hell, what-have-I-got-to-lose, go-for-it, live-for-today, attitude, that their lives would be better. By joining up with someone, the two parts would make a stronger whole. They thought someone else would improve their lives for them.

Warning: Don't let loneliness or feelings of desperation influence your decision making. You can't "fall in love" with someone you've never met. Don't consider moving to another location to be with a new love unless you've known them in person for months or years. Reread the section in Chapter 7 about long-distance relationships. Even if you follow all of the advice in that chapter, deciding to uproot your life and move to another part of the country is risky. We're too old to fail and to have to start over.

And don't allow someone you've known for a short time move to be near you, or worse, to move in with you. Not only might you find you aren't compatible--which could be the least of your concerns—but, they could have evil intentions they've hidden from you.

The January 8, 2003, issue of *The Orange County Register* had a story about a 42-year-old San Clemente woman who met a man on the Internet. E-mails were exchanged for two months before he moved to California and in with her. He smoked, drank and was an angry person. Seven weeks later, she asked him to move out. He allegedly stabbed her to death.

If after these stern words of warning, you still are compelled to uproot your life for the sake of a new love, have the person's background investigated by a professional, as we described in Chapter 4, before proceeding. The chances of a move like the ones described above working out are about 100-to-one.

Fantasy Love

The second situation to avoid is *Fantasy Love,* falling for someone you don't know or barely know. You get so caught up in their looks, you can't think straight. *Fantasy Love* is also referred to as *Instant Chemistry.* You think and believe you're in love, but you're only in lust.

Here's a *Fantasy Love* story a la pastrami. Most deli customers know I write about single life. Instead of paying a shrink big bucks for an hour on the couch, a customer figures he or she can chat for the cost of a sandwich and a bag of chips.

One day, while making a sandwich, a male customer said, "I never thought I could fall in love again at age 54--I mean the head-over-heels type of feeling we knew as kids."

"Mayo and mustard?" I asked.

He said, "I dumped a girlfriend I had a great relationship with, for her."

"Pickle?"

"After eight months, the new one called off the relationship without warning. I'm still devastated."

"Why did you dump the first one?"

"The second one was gorgeous, 17-years-younger."

"A real beauty, huh? To go or are you eating here?"

"I don't know where I went wrong," he said.

"It sounds as if you fell for looks, and didn't evaluate her on more important issues--character, friendship, trust. For her, the in-love feeling must have worn off." (I wanted to tell him the importance of knowing the qualities one seeks in a mate (Chapter 6), but knew he wouldn't hear me.

His mouth was full; he nodded.

"But, you were still in love when she left, and you've been stuck there ever since. Men who date women considerably younger make themselves vulnerable to this type of situation," I said.

He finished his sandwich, thanked me, got into his blue convertible and drove up Pacific Coast Highway. It'll take him awhile to recover. He had not separated the myth of beauty from reality, and loved her as teenagers love. He didn't see that she wasn't right for him.

In chapter 2 of his book, "The Five Love Languages," Gary Chapman discusses mature vs. immature love. He wrote: "Unfortunately, the eternality of the 'in love' experience is fiction, not fact. Dr. Dorothy Tennov, a psychologist, has done long-range studies on the in-love phenomenon. After studying scores of couples, she concluded that the average life span of a romantic obsession is two years."

As we age, we should look at love in a more mature and realistic light. Grown-up love, if you will. Bells and whistles may not go off. Friendship, consideration, appreciation, and being kind to each other should come first and are more important and lasting.

I turned to the next customer, a woman, who said, "Wow, is that guy in the blue car single?"

"Yes, but I don't think he's mentally available," I said.

"Too bad, he's so handsome. I could fall for him, already have." So, the *Fantasy Love* cycle begins again.

Don't expect someone else to improve your life and don't fall for *Fantasy Love*. Each is only short-term.

Chapter 10

Where To Go?

If you're meant to get into a primary relationship again, you'll find your significant other as long as you're 'out there' doing something positive and joyful with your life.

--Barbara Gilvary, Tustin, Calif.

Customers come into my deli or see me around town and say, "You write that dating column don't you?" I smile and say, "You read that?"

They say, "Since you're the dating expert, how do I find a mate?" Then, they step back, cross their arms, and expect in 30 seconds, I can give them an answer that will solve their dating woes forever.

I say, "My middle name isn't Viagra. There's no easy answer, no magic pill, no simple solution on where to meet somebody. What might work for some won't work for others because people have different interests, needs and personalities. No one can give you a simple answer, there isn't one."

The *Where to go?* advice I give is this: people need to get out with people, but they shouldn't go out solely to find a mate. When a person's main motivation in life is that, he or she will come off as desperate and looking too hard. That's a turnoff to other singles and won't work. Besides, we hear most people find someone when they aren't looking.

Instead, people should go out to revitalize their lives and grow, and to experience life. They should go out for themselves and get involved in activities that interest them, and not just in activities where they think they'll meet a mate.

Singles functions

Singles functions are difficult places for older singles to meet potential mates. The ratios are generally so out of kilter, (10:1 or more, women to men), that woman get discouraged. They end up talking only to other women, which isn't what they had hoped to do. Often, men who attend feel so overwhelmed, they slip out the rear exit.

Attending singles functions is fine, but go to them to socialize, make new friends, hear a speaker, or for entertainment. Don't go to them hoping to meet a mate.

For women, the competition at "singles functions" is too great. They need to find other creative outlets—hobbies and activities that interest them--where they also might meet men. Is there something you've always wanted to do but could never find the time? Now's a good time to do it. It's important that your activity places you out among people, and doesn't isolate you. Staying home and spending hours on the computer isolates you.

Where to go?

Here are a few activities to jump start your thinking.

1. Attend reunions and weddings. There's a comfort level about seeing someone you grew up with, or were in love with years ago, or with whom you attended school. By

having backgrounds that touched in some way, you already have a great deal in common.

Weddings and receptions are good places to meet potential mates. Love is in the air. Single people who see happily-wedded couples would like similar happiness for themselves. Meeting someone in a relaxed, jovial atmosphere is easy. Don't be shy. If you see a single you'd like to meet, introduce yourself or ask someone who knows the person to do so. Take *name cards* to reunions and weddings

2. Volunteer. When you help others, you'll feel better about yourself and have a sense of purpose and accomplishment. Where to volunteer depends on what's available where you live. Check local newspapers for organizations that need help. Volunteer at public service television stations. Ginny Reid started a volunteer singles group two years ago in Aliso Viejo, Calif. Now, Ginny's group has more than 75 members. Women outnumber the men, but the group helps at so many functions the women meet men that way. And for single men, volunteering is a terrific way to meet quality women

3. A good way to meet new friends is to have a party where the invited guests are half women and half men, and each guest must bring a member of the opposite sex they aren't dating. When I lived in New York City in the 1960s, a group of us did this and we sure met lots of singles

4. Join a club--ski clubs, sailing clubs, hiking, health clubs, athletic singles clubs, Parents Without Partners, the Sierra

Club, investment clubs, bridge clubs, scrabble groups--to name a few

5. Go back to school. Work toward the degree you never received. Learn a new skill. Stimulate your mind. You'll be around younger people which is refreshing and stimulating. Gina Woodruff, Long Beach, Calif., is taking a screenwriting course, which she's always wanted to do

6. Attend church (It's also good for you). Many have social and singles activities. You're getting out with people and that's important

7. Take dance lessons and go to dances. In some areas, country dancing is popular. You can line dance without a partner. In ballroom dancing, your partner is already in your arms (yippee!). And dancing is good exercise

8. Travel with a group. You'll meet new people. So you won't have to eat alone, hook up at meals or on side trips with a friendly married couple for company. Elderhostels are becoming popular with older singles

9. Take a part-time job where you interface with people. Consider working in retail where men shop

10. "Focus on the right places," says M.P. Wylie, a relationship coach and PHD, Irvine, Calif., "Singles would have a better chance of meeting their life partner. For some, it's church, nature, educational gatherings, family, or a friend's house."

11. Join a support group. Janet Durbin, Steubenville, Ohio, says, "I have a social support group for widows and widowers and many meet at my group and fall in love or find companionship." In Orange County, where I live, the widows and widowers group is called "A New Life" Club. You have to show you're spouse's death certificate to become a member—no party crashers or fakes allowed

12. Go to bookstores. Bigger ones like Barnes and Noble and Borders offer many interesting activities. Check their calendar of events for programs that interest you

13. Start a group as Ginny Reid did. You only need a nucleus of two or three interested people, and one person to "make it happen."

Where the men are...

Remember that Connie Francis hit, "Where the Boys Are?" Now women ask, "Where are the men?" The answer is: Everywhere, but finding "everywhere" is another challenge.

- Some men go to singles dances, but so do ten zillion women. You might meet a guy at one of those home improvement type of places, lots of men wander the aisles, star-struck by their favorite tools. Ask (with a straight-face and a smile), a single-looking guy, something like, "Is this a left-handed screw driver?" Keep your eyes open at any place you shop. Hardware stores, computer stores, and sporting goods outlets have favorable men-to-women ratios.

- Single men golf. Take lessons. Go to a driving range. If a man offers golf pointers, accept them graciously. Give him your name card. If he's married, ask him to introduce you to his single friends (networking). Sign up for mixed foursomes

- Walk your dog everywhere, even near Little League games on Saturday mornings. You'll find divorced dads and widower grandpas along the sidelines. Say something to start a conversation, like "Your grandson played well, will he play in high school?" I know a couple who met at a bark-park (dog-exercise park)

- Single men like delis and car washes. Couples have met in my deli while waiting for an order. Don't make these places your only singles hunting ground, but keep your eyes open when ordering a turkey sandwich. Keep your eyes open whenever you're out in public.

An important point. Don't wait until the last minute to figure out where you're going. Plan your activities in advance, so you don't get caught in the "It's Friday night, where should I go?" situation. That is oh-so discouraging.

In summary, where you go and what you do is up to you. The important thing is to go out to enrich your life and be among people. Be approachable, friendly and yourself.

Chapter 11

Internet Dating

A woman ran a simple ad on the Internet: "Husband wanted." The next day she received 93 e-mails, all from married women, all offering the same thing: "Take mine."

The Internet can be a helpful tool for singles of all ages who are searching for mates.

Some people consider all aspects of middle-age dating demeaning, particularly using the Internet to meet a mate. But, if singles want to hook up, they must make an effort, unless fate simply drops somebody in their lap. The Internet is a valuable resource to consider using.

Internet dating gets mixed reviews. Many singles have had success and swear by it. Others say it's filled with devious people who misrepresent themselves and have evil intentions.

Fact of Internet dating: People will need to provide a recent photo. Few men will continue a conversation with a woman without seeing a picture. And then women have to be prepared for rejection if men don't like what they see (ouch).

Seniors use the Internet

Age doesn't hold back Gini Givan, Baton Rouge, La, from using the Internet. "I'm 75-plus. I've met six older men on the Internet with no bad experiences. After a few e-mails, phone conversations, and a meeting in a public place, judging someone isn't difficult."

Pearl Hedlund, San Antonio, a senior, met George, who lived 70 miles away, over the Internet. They used to drive to a midway point for dates. No more, they're married and travel around the country in a large motor home.

Gale Dundrea, 65, of Leicester, North Carolina, met Ian Kilmer, 67, of Binghamton, NY., online. "Ian's moving south to be with me, and guess what? He proposed. Don't ever say "I'm too old or it will never happen.""

The good—where men outnumber women

"The Internet is one of the few places where single men outnumber single women," says Christine Stieber, of Fullerton, Calif. In her Internet dating classes, Christine (CSTPD@aol.com, 714 792-0115) teaches people how to write profiles and download pictures.

The Internet can be particularly helpful to singles who live in small towns and remote areas or cities where there aren't enough people to date. You meet people online that you wouldn't have otherwise met. Of course, to use the Internet, you need to know how to use a computer and to have access to one.

When people are depressed or lonely, communicating on the Internet can be therapeutic. But, if people are only there for therapy, they waste the time of others who seriously want a mate, so watch out for them.

The bad

The Internet is rife with flakes and fakes. Anybody can be anybody.

--A single man

People often misrepresent themselves on the Internet. "Men want younger women, so I list my age as four years younger than I am. If we go out, I tell them the truth at the end of the date," says Giselle Blum, 61, New Orleans.

Jan Phillips, Tustin, Calif., said, "I won't Internet date—it's too hard to judge honesty, character, etc. I've had friends burned by it. It provides a smoke screen for hiding things like marriages. I know guys who are married or living with someone who use it to liven up their relationship doldrums."

Another woman said, "Even on-line services can be scams. Some want the fee to sign you up, then they say, "there's no one in your area." One I used not only sent me names of people several states away, but in other countries! Also, I asked for men 55-65 and got 20-yr-olds responding!"

Another woman said, "Some on-line dating companies say they'll give you 'one month of free service' before you sign up, but they need your credit card info. Big mistake to give it. With one company, I cancelled before the deadline and they billed me anyway. That wouldn't have been so bad, but the shysters wouldn't remove my charges, telling me I'd gone past the deadline. When I provided the proof, they finally backed down, but what a hassle!!! Anyone who subscribes to this kind of service needs to cover their rear."

People using the Internet can be dishonest about anything and everything. It's easy to have hidden agendas and lives. They can fib about their age, looks, height, weight, availability, goals and where they live.

One woman said, "The Internet is too risky. It's not enjoyable having to be on guard all the time. I've heard that approximately 35 per cent of the males looking for an Internet relationship are married."

Same pickup lines—different women

"I've been on Matchmaker.com for several months and a woman friend suggested that those of us without Friday night dates get together and share our online experiences. We'd create a list of 'good' and 'bad' guys on the site. It's been a learning experience since a lot of us have had responses from the same guys and they use the same pick-up line. It would help us quickly weed-out the 'players,'" said an anonymous woman.

Popular sites

There are over 200 date-matching sites on the Internet. Some will go out of business and new ones will appear on the scene. At the time of this book's printing, these were some of the more popular ones.

Matchmaker.com. Mary Capper, 48, Mission Viejo, Calif, met a man on Matchmaker.com. He works out at her gym but she'd never seen him there, even though they lived in the same area. Matchmaker advertises on TV.

Match.com "I gave Match.com a try. It's great. I went out with 25 very nice, successful men but not the right one. The right one found me, a charming Danish man. This may be a lifetime plan. We are very happy. said Linda Anton, 54, and Steen Brydum (the Danish man), Dana Point, Calif.

Love@aol.com Linda Jay, of Marin County, north of San Francisco, e-mailed, "I lost my first husband in 1994. I met a man thru aol who had moved to Marin from Miami about three years ago. We married. I felt comfortable meeting him online because I had met my first husband thru computer dating, in 1969, in Boston."

ThirdAge.com is a free website for people 50-plus that sends out members' profiles to other singles. Linda Hansen of Chattanooga, Tenn., had given up on the Internet when thirdage.com sent her profile to a man in her area. They talked on the phone for two months before meeting. While proceeding slowly, she's thrilled she didn't delete him and that ThirdAge matched them up.

Others: **Yahoo.com, KISS.com and Digitalcity.com**

A few cautions

If your e-mail address reveals your true name, have an unlisted telephone number. Don't give out your street address, and be discreet with your phone number.

Karen Robinson, of Rancho Santa Margarita, Calif, made a valid point: "Many singles are afraid of meeting some psycho on the Internet, well, I could meet him in the grocery store." Karen's right, but please refer to *When Meeting Strangers* in the beginning of Chapter 4, about precautions to take when meeting strangers.

When you haven't met someone face-to-face, chemistry isn't predictable. Many of the precautions mentioned in Chapter 7 about long-distance relationships also apply to e-mail relationships. Don't establish an e-mail relationship for too long before you've had a face-to-face meeting. Until you do, you're only dealing with fantasies, hopes and a false sense of closeness.

If you wait too long to meet in person, a face-to-face meeting could be uncomfortable if the chemistry and attraction aren't there. You may have disclosed too much about yourself and you'll feel awkward. Not to mention the time you've wasted.

And don't do what one woman did. *The Orange County Register* featured a front page story on January 10, 2003, about a California mother who met a North Carolina man on the Internet. She left her two children--one age seven, one four--to take care of themselves *alone* for three weeks. *The Register* stated, "She was charged with two counts of felony child endangerment and is being held on $50,000 bail." The police also discovered she had done the same thing two months before when she went to London for two weeks. Can you imagine? Loneliness can make monsters out of people.

The Internet is a high-risk, high-potential-return investment of your time. Consider making it a marketing tool in your mate-seeking plan.

In the next chapter, we look at two other dating tools— using personal ads and dating services.

Chapter 12

Personal Ads and Dating Services

Personal ads and dating services are among the many tools singles can use to meet other singles. Personal ads can be particularly useful for older singles, those in their 60s and above. The cost is reasonable, and unlike the Internet, personal ads don't require the use of a computer. The ads zero-in on a specific location and people write copy tailored to their needs. They select the people with whom they want to meet. And when first talking on the phone, a person will be judged on personality, voice and attitude, and not on looks. No photo is required.

Some people feel using personal ads is demeaning, but use of them should be viewed as merely another mate-seeking tool.

Laura Hughes' use of personal ads was so thorough, it's been included here as a guide for others. Many singles in their 60-80s give up hope of finding another partner. Not Laura. The Portland, Oregon, woman had been happily married for 48 years before she was widowed. She hoped to find another partner, but hadn't met anyone compatible through introductions by friends, taking college classes and joining an over-40's singles dance club.

With the encouragement of her two daughters and other older single women friends, Laura put a personal ad in the *Portland Oregonian* newspaper. Beforehand, she listed the qualities she hoped for in a mate, which helped her write a more effective ad. "I refined my list, and changed later ads when I found that some things didn't seem as important as others," said Laura.

"I ran three ads in the senior section over four months and had 61 responses to my recorded message, which said they needn't say much because I'd call everyone who left their phone number."

Laura didn't give out her number and had her number blocked when she called the men. A few men made inappropriate remarks, but most were nice. Laura met 40 for coffee or lunch, but only made more dates with six.

"I paid for extra words in the last ad, to tell more about myself and the qualities I sought. I had fewer responses, but we were better matched. The 40th and last was Jack Hughes, a 72-year-old widower, who himself had met 'about 25' women answering ads.

"When Jack and I met for lunch, he wanted to quickly put me at ease by showing me his I.D as a retired Los Angles P.D. officer. Our three-hour conversation was the longest either of us had during an initial meeting. By that time, we knew we were pretty compatible and very attracted to each other. Even though we had political and religious differences, we both were accepting and respectful of the other's views."

On their fourth date, Jack took her to a grandson's wedding. "It was apparent that he had an exceptionally close relationship with his three (step) children and six grandchildren, which made me even more sure he might be the right one for me.

"Two weeks later, on our 10th date, he proposed and three months later, we married."

Laura and Jack bought a condominium in a retirement community in southern California and now live near Jack's three children and six other grandchildren.

Laura said, "I encourage others who have lost a spouse after a long, happy marriage to try to find another with whom to again share your life."

An anonymous woman said, "I'm a 53-year-old divorced woman (15 years). I recently moved to a new city. A girlfriend suggested I advertise in the local personals. After dating several men, I met a wonderful match for me. He's 58, a widower. We live together and couldn't be happier. We have the same interests and dislikes. If you keep yourself out there and try to meet other singles, you'll have a success story also."

And this from Helen, "For single women over 55, one of the best ways to meet the opposite sex is a classified ad. If you aren't a tall, thin blond and you look your age, the chances are that men aren't going to fall over themselves asking you to dance.

"With an ad, you talk to them on the phone without them making a judgment about how you look. At least that way they can find that you have some interesting things to say and maybe something in common. If you like what they say on the phone, have a short meeting.

"I put ads in the singles column three times and met many nice men. A year ago, a wonderful man answered my ad and we are now engaged. If I hadn't placed an ad, our paths wouldn't have crossed. Doing a classified ad doesn't take much effort for the rewards you can get. It's a safe easy way to meet nice people (As a reminder, refer to the warning in Chapter 4 about meeting strangers).

When drafting personal ads

-Write about what you want, not what you dislike
-Use humor, correct spelling and grammar
-Describe your interests and passions
-Be honest and positive

-Learn from online dating sites. See what words they recommend and insert them in your personal ads. Once your ad is running, adjust it based on the responses you receive

An example of a good and a bad ad

Good ad: "Lovely happy lady 5'4" seeking a gentleman who enjoys dancing, movies and travel. Someday, I'd love to see Paris, with a compatible mate."

Bad ad: "Rescue me. Fresh out of abusive relationship. Ugly divorce. I need to be treated like a queen. Still a little in shock."

Dating Services

Using a dating service to meet potential mates is another available option. Dating services vary by city.

People usually hire dating services because they don't have time to look on their own, or they're unsure of where else to look. They're often willing to pay big bucks. They want to be selective and feel a dating service will screen potential mates for them.

Types of Dating Services

1. Matching Services based on data members provide

Based on the profiles members fill out, matches are generated most likely by computer. When the computer finds a potential match, each party is notified, and the rest is up to the two people. Biggest complaint: computer-generated matches overlook the human element. *It's Just Lunch* is an example of this type of service.

2. Video Dating Services

This type of service is time consuming. You fill out a profile and are videotaped. Then, you go through the service's library of photos and videos and select matches.

The company does the contacting for you. It could take weeks for the other person to respond; they have to come in and view your video and photos. This method puts a great deal of emphasis on looks, and as we age, we don't like that. Some don't get selected. Wow, speaking of rejection, that would be horrible.

And depending on the service, some charge extra for the videoing and require an updated video each year, which could add more expense.

Great Expectations and *Heart to Heart* are well-known video dating services.

3. Personal Matchmakers

Members are matched by an actual human being (imagine that) who knows both parties. This is a more personal and effective method, but these types of services are expensive. Selective Search of Chicago is an example.

4. Combination Services

These services use a combination of the above three. They try to use the best of video, matching, testing and putting the right people together. Members make the decision on whether to meet someone. These can also be expensive. *Intouch Dating International*, in southern California, is an example

One woman's experience

Not all experiences with dating services are favorable. Cheri, age 53, was so upset with a dating service, she shared the details.

"I spent 3 hours in their office--personality tests, long discussions about preferences, etc. I didn't know until later that their 'fee' is based on your income and all those 'tests,' and that their show of sincerity are sales pitches. I paid $3,290, in full, on my credit card. (Very dumb, I could have paid in increments, and later stopped more payments).

"I requested someone FUN, who liked to drink socially, who was free to go anywhere, and liked nice cars. The matches were nowhere near the mark. I'd been scammed."

Cheri had her attorney write the service a letter but got no response. She complained to the Better Business Bureau, the Attorney General's office, the local Police Department Fraud Division and the county's District Attorney's office. "Their reply to the Attorney General's office was that I was too picky and hadn't given them a chance and that their contract was 'air tight,'" said Cheri. There had been seven complaints against the company in two years. She decided going to court wasn't worth it.

"I still get letters from them stating: 'We know you're disappointed, but we pride ourselves on making our clients happy. Would you like to unfreeze your membership? Yeah, right. Did Charlie Manson just get paroled?" Cheri said, "You can't buy love!! Or fun, for that matter!"

What others say

Pat said, "I was offered a free membership in 'a well known' service. My instructions were not to spend too much time on the phone but make a date and take the woman to dinner. It was stressed to me that there were an abundance of women who had paid big bucks to be in this service but few men.

"I was fired from my 'free job' because I wouldn't cooperate. I wanted a picture of a potential date, but was told it wasn't possible, the ladies were paying to be discreet. I think the services are a joke. Save your money ladies and join a gym."

John said, "I tried two dating services a couple of years ago and found them to be a rip-off, particularly for older people. All they were interested in was signing me up and getting the fee."

Theresa said, "Be absolutely positive what you're getting for your money. Don't be suckered in. Stay totally unemotional because you could get similar, local men through an online service for far less. "I called two of the local dating services. You paid $100 to meet ten men. Totally absurd. The men were probably paid by the agency".

Janet Frey, Garden Grove, Calif., said, "I've been a member (of Great Expectations) since 1989 and have met some nice people but no love connection yet. It does make me feel good to know something about people before I go out with them."

William, Denver, said, "I was pressured to join at a discount since I wasn't sure. After signing, I was advised not to be too restrictive. I had asked for non-smokers and someone short (I'm 5'2"). The woman told me in America women are not as willing to go out with someone my size as they are in Europe. In the book, all women had requested someone at least 5'6". The woman said I should keep coming back to see book updates. I ended my experience and lost $500. It's all lip-service till they get your money."

Judy S., San Clemente, Calif., said, "I've worked at two dating services. The difficult part was meeting many of the clients' unrealistic expectations. If a client is a "3" or "4" on the attractive scale, inevitably they want a potential mate who's a "10." Most of the "10's" want someone with money. If a woman or man was not young, beautiful or slender, often they were overlooked.

"It's true that once some dating services get money, they don't care about their clients. I worked for a man whose agenda was personal, to date all the lovely young ladies. It was a bit sleazy to me."

Dating Service Cost

Most dating services charge from $500 to $5000, depending on how much "service" you want. You can spend more. Fees for "It's Just Lunch" start at approximately $1000. For Great Expectations, $1900 or so, (may not include cost of video services).

Selective Search charges a yearly retainer fee of $15,000 to $25,000.

One service, claiming to be in Beverly Hills, had this message on their website: "XXX receives up to $200,000 per client, depending on geographic location and desired selection criteria." For that price, maybe they'll fix you up with the King of Siam or a rich Saudi prince. Be very leery.

What to watch out for

- Being mislead during the sales (recruitment) process. They love you, you're the best, you're going to have a lot of dates. Remember, these are just strokes to make you feel good and sign up for expanded services
- Read the fine print of the contract. Know how and be able to terminate the deal if you aren't satisfied
- Don't pay with a credit card or sign multi-year deals
- Don't expect too much. Ask for references.
- Find out how many members are actually active

Dating services are only as good as the clients they sign up. Many have bad reputations and most are expensive. Before committing, investigate other options for meeting potential mates. Remember Cheri's words, "You can't buy love!! Or fun, for that matter."

Chapter 13

Sex

At a potluck dinner in a retirement community, a little old lady raised her fist and shouted, "Any man who guesses what's in my hand can have sex with me tonight." A gentleman in the back of the room yelled, "An elephant!" "Close enough," she said.

Janet Durbin, age 63, of Steubenville, Ohio, asked, "Is it okay at our age to have our sox knocked off?" The answer: "you betcha." Sex is enjoyable and can be good for your health. The Jan/Feb, 2003, issue of *AARP Modern Maturity Magazine* had an article in the Navigator section entitled, "Sexual Healing: Why a romp in the sack is great medicine." The content of the article suggests that sex can be healthy for seniors.

BUT, NOT SO FAST. As in many aspects of dating later in life, one has to be careful.

A 51-year-old divorcee named Gail went to Las Vegas for a friend's wedding. Her dating service put her in touch with "a really nice guy" who lived there. Gail and the man exchanged telephone conversations and e-mails before she arrived. They agreed to go out on a date.

Gail said they did the tourist type of things at the new hotels—including a visit to the art gallery at the Bellagio—and then had dinner at a buffet. At his request, they went Dutch, which was also what Gail wanted.

They were the same age. Gail was pleased because he was well-mannered and a good conversationalist, had a master's degree and said he was the son of a retired Air Force officer. She thought he might be a good mate for her.

Halfway through dinner, he leaned forward at the table and said, "I find you very attractive and want to sleep with you tonight."

Gail said, "It was kind of like, pass the salt, let's get it on." She began laughing, composed herself and said, "You're kidding, right?"

"No, I'm serious. I thought I'd have a 50-50 chance."

"Your percentages are way off—it's a one-hundred percent no."

In the hotel lobby, he kissed her on the cheek, said he enjoyed her company and maybe they'd see each other again. They didn't.

Single women need to be prepared when faced with a situation like Gail's. The guy didn't want a relationship. All he wanted was to take her to bed. Unfortunately, there are a lot of horny men age-60 and older like the Vegas guy. When you meet one, do as Gail did, keep your respect and get out of the situation as quickly as possible. Don't buy into romantic, first-night lines. If anybody tries to rush sex, don't. It's too dangerous.

Sex is a difficult issue because most of us enjoy intimacy and want it to be a part of our relationship.

With sex, there are risks, even at our age. And it's alarming that the fastest-growing segment of the population to contact HIV and STDs (sexually transmitted diseases) is age 50-plus. The Centers for Disease Control and Prevention (CDC) reports that in 1999, 13.4 percent of the new AIDS cases in this country involved people age 50 and older.

Statistics don't reflect the real picture. Since seniors aren't likely to be tested for HIV or AIDS, there are some walking around with the disease and unaware of it, and not included in the above statistic.

The CDC reports that as of November 29, 2002, the cumulative number of reported AIDS cases totals 816,149 in the United States, since AIDS was discovered in 1981. That's *reported* AIDS cases, not just HIV cases. Over **90,000** of those are people who were over age 50 when diagnosed.

Here's a frightening statistic. According to the July 21, 2000, *The Orange County Register*, in an article entitled, "Condom Report Raises Debate," written by Will Dunham, "Sexually transmitted diseases, including HIV, affect more than 65 million Americans." (That's almost one third of all Americans). And in the same article, Dunham wrote, "Condoms effectively prevent HIV transmission but data is lacking on whether they work to block most sexually transmitted diseases."

One of my women readers shared this, "HPV is another nasty virus…Genital Warts…condoms cannot guarantee protection. Just touching someone who has this will transport it, even shaking hands can do it. I should know, I got it from my husband who cheated on me often." Can you imagine how angry and betrayed this woman must feel?

Most older people don't worry about the risks

There is a feeling among people over 50 that having sex is worry-free, that they aren't at risk. After all, the women are likely too old to get pregnant, which at one time in their lives was their biggest worry about having sex. Many feel HIV happens only to younger, more promiscuous people, and only affects gay men and people who live in Africa. With performance-enhancing pills, sex is happening more often than before. Some people have multiple sex partners.

HIV is devious. Symptoms can take up to ten years to appear. If you have questions about the use of condoms or reducing the risks of contacting HIV or other STDs, contact the CDC National AIDS Hotline at 1-800-342-2437 or on the web at www.cdc.gov. The CDC provides information on safe sex practices and risk factors for HIV. The CDC continually updates information through new studies and findings. Here are the risk factors.

The Risk Factors

- The biggest risk factor is unprotected sex, heterosexual or otherwise
- A little known risk factor includes any person who had a blood transfusion prior to 1985, before donated blood was tested for HIV/AIDS. So, you could meet a person who had a transfusion in 1984 from a traffic accident, and they could be infected. Scary stuff
- Having two or more sex partners in one year
- Sharing needles

Practice Safe Sex

According to the CDC, the most reliable way to avoid transmission of STDs and HIV is to abstain from sexual intercourse (i.e., oral, vaginal, or anal sex) or to be in a long-term, mutually monogamous relationship with an uninfected partner. The CDC also states:

- Both partners should get tested for STDs, including HIV, before initiating sexual intercourse (But the scary thing about testing is the antibodies may not show up until six months after sexual contact was made. So a guy could show you his HIV test to prove you can have safe sex and yet be infected).

- If a person chooses to have sexual intercourse with a partner whose infection status is unknown or who is infected with HIV or another STD, a new (latex) condom should be used for each act of insertive intercourse.

Sex is alive and well among seniors

In the September-October, 1999, issue of *Modern Maturity*, in an article called "The Facts Of Life: Everything you wanted to know about sex (after 50)," writer Ken Budd raised and answered seven questions about sex. Mr. Budd indicated that seniors who have been sexually active usually will continue being that way, although the sex drive may lessen a bit. He wrote that sex contributes to living longer and people can resume sexual activity after recovering from heart problems.

Three readers share their opinions on sex

Why can't two people meet for drinks or dinner without the expectations that sex should follow?

-- Column reader Marie, Newport Beach, Calif.

Bruce Boycks, Laguna Beach, Calif., said, "Believe it or not, most guys will not go to bed with just anyone. Be thankful when a guy expresses interest, it could be a compliment." Bruce makes a point, but notice he says 'could be a compliment.' Even if it is a compliment, that doesn't mean you hop into the sack.

One 46-year-old male said, "After the sex--if we enjoyed each other being together--then I will want to get to know her with the intention of building a long-term relationship." Most women would say his statement puts the cart before the horse. Sorry sir, it doesn't work that way.

An Indianapolis widow said, "I have chosen not to date because every male I've had a conversation with cannot believe someone would choose to live without sex if they could live otherwise. Somehow, in considering if I want to have dinner or go to a movie, crawling into bed is not one of the first things I would think of. If men want meaningful relationships, why can't they give you time to get to know them before wanting to jump your bones? I think all of the men over 50 I've met are on performance-enhancing pills and want to try it on someone."

What to do if a man wants sex too soon

"As soon as I see it coming and I have no reciprocal interest, it ends the relationship. I usually try to deflect the comments about sex and just don't return calls. It's probably not the most mature thing to do, but the easiest. I'm not sure they need/deserve an explanation, nor do I think it would change their modus operandi. A horn dog is a horn dog. I don't think you can change another person," said Sandra of Detroit.

"Some men think the price of dinner includes a show. That's why all of my dates are in a restaurant or very public place for at least the first three or more. I simply tell the men that I'm not one to sleep together on the first few dates," says Patricia, Fairbanks, Alaska.

An anonymous woman said, "With a smile, move slightly away and say, 'I'm not into that.' Explain briefly what you are looking for--friendship, possible romance (later)...The men who want to go to bed fast aren't the ones you want."

"Ask to meet his mother first. If he has no interest in introducing you to the significant people in his life, he will probably run after getting what he wants. Asking to meet his mom may make him run sooner, but then you can laugh about it instead of crying (later)," suggests Gina Woodruff, 37, Long Beach, Calif.

Patty, a woman who loves horses, says, "I take it as a compliment to my sexual presence, tip my cowboy hat, and say, 'Thank you. I'll let you know when I'm ready.' If they won't accept that, I get rough."

Another said, "Tell him, 'I'm an affectionate, warm and passionate woman. If we become a couple, I'll enjoy sharing those things with you."

Final thoughts on sex

Sex with a stranger puts both people at risk and has no meaning. It's too dangerous. Neither knows with whom the other has been. What if somebody has a disease? It's not worth the risk. If people still have sex with strangers, at the very least, they will worry until the test results come back. That's no fun.

To avoid men who are only looking for sex, be careful when meeting a stranger in a bar or when "meeting for a drink." A coffee date or lunch is better. Meeting someone through your church or while doing volunteer work should be a safer bet also.

I'm not an expert on sex. This book is not a manual on sex. It's intention isn't to ruin your sexual enjoyment, but only to make you aware of the dangers involved and how to deal with some of the pitfalls you could face, similar to what Gail faced in the opening story of this chapter.

Mark Victor Hansen, the Co-creator of the #1 *New York Times* best-selling series "Chicken Soup For The Soul®" (82 million copies sold) and Co-author of "The One Minute Millionaire," in an exclusive interview, told me this about older adults: "About gray power--no one should give up their sex life or their life at all."

Mark's right, yes, as we get older, we have the right to enjoy sex, to have "our socks knocked off." But, we need to do so safely.

Chapter 14

Living Arrangements

I scratch my head in amazement when I read about people moving in together after a few dates. I seldom get past a second date and a kiss standing outside the door. I guess I travel in the SLOW crowd, or maybe I should stop dating women who belong to "Platonic's Anonymous."

--Joe F, Los Angeles

You never thought you'd meet someone again, but it's happened. You've been together long enough to know you're committed, hopefully, for the rest of your lives. But you live in separate residences. You're always together, either at his house or yours. Living under the same roof makes sense. What should you do? Live together? Get married? Co-mingle assets? These are tough and important questions. There's no right answer, it depends on the two individuals and what's best for them. Whatever the decision, it shouldn't be taken lightly. Failing again at our age takes a heavy toll. Let's look at the options.

Living Together?

Deciding to live together is a decision that shouldn't be rushed. Even when people have dated for a long period of time, deciding to live together--under any arrangement--is a major lifestyle adjustment that can change a relationship, sometimes for the worse.

Before living together, couples need to communicate. They must be honest with each other. Both must make expectations, motives and reservations clear. This isn't a time for hidden agendas or making assumptions. If one party doesn't express an expectation because she or he is afraid the other won't agree, problems will likely follow. For example, If a guy expects his partner to cook for him, and she's thinking they'll eat out often, resentment will build.

Before moving in, (even before getting involved), both people should express their long-term goals. Does one or the other want marriage?

All issues need to be resolved beforehand. Don't leave anything open-ended. Don't say, "We'll decide on that if and when it comes up."

Don't live together for the wrong reasons. Saving money is a great benefit, but it shouldn't be why you live together, unless you plan only to be roommates and not lovers. Agree on the financial arrangements beforehand.

Don't make a lifestyle change because it's convenient or if you aren't compatible.

In whose house to live? That's up to the couple to decide. It's important that both parties can feel at home, regardless of whose house, or if it's a neutral house. Be sure there's enough "space" for both of you. If you're too tightly thrown together, friction could start.

If it's your home, don't let a loser move in, even "for just a few days." Trust your instincts. If you have doubts ahead of time, don't proceed. And if you're the person moving, be sure you're doing the right thing and have a back-up plan if moving-in doesn't work. If you own a home, and if it's financially possible, keep the house and rent it, just in case you need to move back later. Besides, real estate appreciation is generally one of the better investments.

Should middle age singles marry again?

I want to meet someone and get married. I'm not crazy about the living together stuff. I guess I have old values.

--Janet Frey, Garden Grove, Calif.

What women say

Janet Durbin shared, "I'm planning to marry my best friend next year. We met in my widows group several years ago and I finally realized he drove me crazy for a reason, I cared for him more than I wanted to admit. The wonderful Social Security laws won't allow us to get married sooner and maybe that's OK. We both have houses and have gone the gambit on where we'll live. I'm selling my home, his is much nicer. I never thought at age 64 I would be worrying about health insurance, his money, my money, his kids, my kids, his house, my house, his furniture, my furniture--sure makes a person tired, but if you care enough, you'll get thru the legal hassles and hopefully live happily ever after."

Becky Cook, 53, Lake Forest, Calif., ended a two-year relationship because marriage wasn't in the picture. "Without the marriage commitment, a person is just playing house and can leave whenever he feels the need to do so. I don't want to be a girlfriend the rest of my life. If he's in love with me, he will give me a ring and a wedding date."

Another woman, Leslie, said she plans to remarry in the near future. "I will start the adventure of finding a man who

113

has a similar vision and unite in the quest of sharing life's peak moments."

Since Leslie plans to remarry soon, I asked if she had a guy picked out. She doesn't, but added, "I have my list of non-negotiable criteria, and from now on all the men I meet will be evaluated to see if they are candidates."

A friend of mine is busy raising four children on her own. She says she wouldn't live with someone or marry at this stage in her life. "I'd live separately, give each other space, a lot of respect, love, and trust." Last I heard, my friend is considering marrying a new man she met. Love can move mountains and change people's minds.

Some women would test the waters before marrying. "I would live with him for at least a year. At our age, we are set in our ways, and I would want to make sure our lifestyles would mesh. Who wants to grow old alone? NOT ME!" said Cari Magnan, 53, San Clemente, Calif.

Ivory Dorsey, Atlanta, Georgia, said, "I would not consider marrying a man who isn't financially mature—it's a sure formula for disaster (been there-done that)."

Kris Miller of San Francisco said no to marriage. "Forget about marriage. Life is more fun on the edge. Someone told me once that marriage is for children. I didn't understand it at the time, but it's become clear," Kris makes a valid point. If people aren't going to have children, one of the reasons to remarry is eliminated.

One woman said, "I knew a couple who lived together for 16 years, got married and divorced five years later."

Many people who have been married twice or more, don't want another marriage. The reasons sited most: protection of assets and property, and legal hassles.

MSNBC.com reported on May 24, 2002: "The largest growing sector of people living together without being married is people over 40. In fact 11 million people nationwide have made this their decision."

Southern California men on marrying again

Joe Monge of Dana Point has been married twice, once for eight years, the other for ten. "I'm 48 and concerned about having enough money to retire on. I'm involved with a 44-year-old woman with two children. We get along better than in either of my marriages. However, I'm not looking to marry again," said Joe.

I told Joe I'd like to quote him, but I didn't want to get him in trouble with his girlfriend. "No problem in quoting me," he said, it will save me from having to bring up the subject. I'll just show her your book!"

Singles admit to loneliness. Barry Eng of Irvine explained that his lifestyle has kept him single. He's traveled extensively throughout Asia, and worked in Taiwan for three years. "I've always wanted to meet someone to hopefully marry," said Barry, "and I confess I've often had to deal with the heartaches of loneliness."

Elliott Ryal, age 62, Norwalk, was married 38 years when he became a widower. He would remarry, but fears getting hurt again. Elliott says the person he falls in love with and marries needs to promise that she won't die before he does.

`Patrick Freeman, Laguna Beach, describes himself as "age 59 feeling 20." Regarding marriage, Patrick said,

"Why screw up a good relationship by putting the pressures of marriage on it? I mean delay marriage until distracting influences like teenagers are out of the house-- not putting it off forever but until the distractions and roadblocks to happiness are somewhat minimized. Marriage can be an excuse to stop growing personally. I will never make that mistake again."

Ron Weil of Vista would consider marriage "very strongly," but he added, "I would not want to lose my home again, and have to leave with only my dog, a futon and my vegetable juicing machine. I think in today's society, true love and a content and fulfilling marriage are fleeting fantasies."

William Mosconi of Anaheim e-mailed: "Just living together is not committing to the relationship. It has a temporary attitude about it, and if something happens that you aren't in agreement with, you can just pull out without making an effort to see it through. However, if a relationship isn't working, being married doesn't mean a piece of paper will make it work."

If people decide to marry, they should consider a **pre-nuptial** agreement. Each person should be represented by different lawyers. I've seen hastily-drawn agreements backfire. If a proposed marriage is open and free, a pre-nuptial shouldn't be viewed as a sign of distrust, but of both parties being intelligent. Done right, pre-nuptials will protect assets brought into the marriage.

People planning to marry should know the tax consequences in the state where they'll live.

Also, those bound for the altar should be careful if they hire a wedding planner. The *Orange County Register* reported on July 14, 1999, that a Laguna Beach wedding planner went out of business and cost ten brides between $17,000 and $40,000 each. Plan your own wedding. It will be more personal and less expensive.

Some people will only live together (and some will only have sex together), if they are married. They say their religious or personal beliefs influence them. I respect their beliefs. If that's how they feel, that's their right.

The divorce rate for second and third marriages exceeds 70 percent. If you're planning to remarry, be sure you know what you're getting into. And what about the assets? We discuss them next.

To co-mingle funds or not?

Should middle-aged singles--who've likely been married before--co-mingle assets with a new love?

A Chicago woman e-mailed "In my marriage, I wasn't allowed to have my name on any financial papers or documents—not even the check book. I never knew how much my husband earned until we were divorced.

"Four years after going through a really ugly marriage and divorce, and now very secure in my own right, I'm faced with learning to trust a lovely man. There is no way I would lose myself in another manipulation.

"He and I have talked about the financial end and we both agree in the event of marriage there would be a prenuptial agreement. When he recognized my reservations concerning mingling money, he suggested…"

When I wrote about her in my newspaper column, I cut off her quote there because I was concerned about her co-mingling money. She dug her way out before and is reopening the chance of having financial problems again.

Charlene Hill, of Tustin, Calif., shared her experience and opinion, "I was married for seven years. Went into it completely in love and full of trust. I ended up losing my home in San Juan Capistrano of 19 years, as well as my inheritance--about $330,000 overall. Don't co-mingle monies!"

Cheryl Wilson, Redmond, Wash., said, "I'm in total agreement about not co-mingling your money if you choose to get married. Healthy people don't need to co-mingle money."

And San Antonio's Pearl Hedlund, who remarried, says, "Keep your name and your assets in your name—and split all expenses."

Sandi Benson of Tustin, Calif., said, "Have you hit a sore spot with me! I have huge money issues. I was married to a controlling spouse. When I told him I wanted a divorce, he went into my wallet when I wasn't looking and took all my credit cards and my checkbook. I too have clawed my way back from having nothing." Sandi said if she remarries, she'd share one account to pay bills and that's it. Her assets would stay in her name.

"Pressing the issue to join in 'financial matrimony' is of a control nature. I wouldn't allow someone to dictate what I spend my money on. I want to know what my half of the monthly budget is and I will plan accordingly," said Janet Thomas of Omaha, Nebraska.

If someone controls your money, they control you. If a potential mate protests too loudly about keeping funds separate, consider that a red flag and rethink the relationship. Usually, the person who protests is the person with fewer assets.

Most people feel if they live with someone or remarry later in life, a joint account is okay, but the rest of the assets should be kept separate. Mimi Fane, Tustin, Calif., who has sponsored successful Orange County singles dances for years, says when she and a male friend dated, they would each put money into what they called "The Wallet," and all shared expenses came out of it. When it was empty, they replenished "The Wallet." What a great idea!

Evaluate living arrangements carefully

Decisions on living arrangements are of major importance. Think them through carefully. People often act too quickly out of loneliness, only to regret it later. We're too old to start over again, or to have to dig ourselves out of a hole we didn't need to be in.

Living together is a good way to test the waters, but many people feel it's leaves the door too wide open for people to bail out. And marrying again? You'd better be positive before taking that step. And for heaven's sake, don't co-mingle your funds. Love and share and give to each other, but protect what you have.

Chapter 15

When Children are Involved

I have six children, ages 6 to 19, do I even get to consider myself available? I'm incredibly lonely.

--divorced woman after 17 years of marriage

One of the challenging issues for middle-age singles is dating when children are a consideration. Can it work? It's a complex issue, each situation is different. The combination of scenarios and problems is as mind-boggling as arranging the letters in a can of alphabet soup.

When children are still at home

Having a relationship while raising children is difficult for a single parent. One single mom said, "A love life with children at home requires too much time and too many locked doors."

The kids need to be the top priority, and it's the exceptional person who can make the children and the mate both feel special. Take the woman in the opening quote above. Not too many men are going to get involved with someone with six children. And how would she find time to date? Can you imagine the guy picking her up at her house? He'd have to wear full body armor to avoid the scrutiny, barbs, tricks and antics from the kids.

Vi, 40, a native of Viet Nam, has five girls—one in college, two in high school, one age 10 and one nine. She ended a relationship with a man who wanted to marry her and have children. She felt he didn't care enough about her children. "When we rented movies, he got ones that interested him and didn't consider whether the kids would enjoy them. I want a man who accepts and cares about my children."

Then Vi met Matthew, 39, who had never been married. They've dated a couple of years. "I love this man," says Vi, "he is great with my children. He helps with their homework and takes the whole bunch of us out to dinner. We plan to marry. He wants to help raise my children and the kids are crazy about him."

In another case, a single mom with two early-teenage children explains why she ended a two-year relationship: "I don't love anyone enough to displace the lives of my children. My boyfriend felt that the partner comes before children, parents or extended family. Even though ending the relationship was painful and took its toll, I could not accept his premise," she said

For single moms, it's tough. Rose has two children. For five years, she's dated a divorcee who also supports two children. She wants to marry him, but says, "I'm not pressuring marriage. He is good to the children. Sometimes, his expectations are unrealistic. He expects their bedrooms to be immaculate and their plates completely cleaned after dinner. Reality for a single working mom is coming home tired and just wanting peace and quiet. One must bend the rules in order to maintain sanity. The guilt is what gets me. I think it's unfair for the children not to have a dad. My life is a soap opera, only I cannot turn it off."

Men who date women with children at home must be prepared to make sacrifices.

Burl Estes, Mission Viejo, Calif, said, "Several women I

dated had children who were resentful. Take a guess with whom those women sided? The relationships were doomed from the start." Burl explained how his present girlfriend's 13 and 17-year-olds have come to tolerate him. "I have a way of dealing with them. I'll say: 'Stop that or we'll bond and become friends.' It works like magic." Burl has been with Gina ten years and he says he has a wonderful relationship with her children.

I've never had children of my own, but twice lived with women who did. In both relationships, before living together, I underestimated the affect of living with kids. Naïvely, I figured I could handle anything, and didn't think much about it beforehand, but the kids turned out to be a big challenge and put stress on the relationship. "You're not my dad," I heard more than once.

David Gerard lives in Burlington, Ontario, Canada. He has two children from his first marriage. He sees them on Wednesday nights and three weekends a month. He and his second wife are separating and he's taking care of their 4-year-old and their twins (2 ½). David says, "The kids are my primary concern…dating will have to take a back seat for now."

Adult children can interfere

David Silver, of Elberon, New Jersey, a DePauw University classmate of mine, explained why a four-year relationship ended.

"The key reason: she insisted on being more important to me than my children. I offered her a place of equal importance—everybody number one—but that wasn't good enough, and it began to get in the way.

"These are grown children (youngest is 19), and she insisted on parenting them whenever we were together. I quit parenting them years ago, and simply try to be their friend, which seems to work much better."

Once out of the roost, kids shouldn't interfere with single parents' relationships. They should want their parents to be happy and enjoy themselves.

Betty Clark, Pontiac, Michigan, married a man 16-years-older than she. Betty wrote: "He had a daughter two-years-younger than I. That was the only problem we had that made any difference. The children were jealous, but it worked anyway because we were devoted. Still, the children never accepted that their father 'had a life.'"

The kids aren't always at fault for being involved. Some parents hold on too long and won't let go of their children. Some let their kids tell them whom they should date. Others even blame their breakups on children, while masking the true reasons their relationships didn't work.

Some kids interfere on purpose. They're suspicious of the new love's motivation. They fear that mom or dad is so enthralled over the new love that they will be disinherited. I have friends where that has happened. The new wife gets everything, and the kids get snubbed. Of course, people have their reasons, and it's none of my business, but in a couple of cases, it seemed unfair to me.

Sometimes kids need to return home to live with mom or dad. That's understandable. But, if the stay goes on and on without some sort of a "move out" date, it could affect the parent's relationship. Some parents allow their children who are in their 30s and 40s (even 50s) to move back in permanently. Perhaps they had a drug habit and have no money, or they can't keep a job, or they just had bad luck. They need mom or dad's help. By allowing the adult child to stay forever, the parent becomes an enabler to that child's bad habits. They aren't doing the child any favors and could lose a relationship at the same time. Difficult to force a child out, but sometimes it has to be done. Richard Sacks, of Huntington Beach, Calif., said, "All I meet are women who've been married twice and molly-coddle their age 23 to 30 kids at home."

If you have children, and are involved, or seeking a relationship, try David Silver's suggestion, make everybody number one.

Cheri, 53, wrote: "I've been in a five-year relationship. Unfortunately, it's coming to an end and one of the main reasons is children. My boyfriend made it perfectly clear there is no way my son could live with us." She moved out.

After a few weeks of trying the singles scene, her ex-fiancé offered to change if she would marry him, which she did.

"Things have gone pretty well," says Cheri, "but my son again may need to live with us and my husband still says no. Will be interesting to see how it all turns out."

They married without resolving the problem of the possibility of the son coming to live with them. Her fiancé offered to change, but didn't. Potential conflicts over children's issues should be resolved before a major step like marriage.

"Once the kids have moved out, a parent must make a

conscious choice of whether or not to let the kids interfere with a relationship. Some parents help their children so much they don't let the kids be adults," says Greta Cohn, of San Clemente, Calif., a mother of four and grandmother of eight, who loves her children, but raised them to be independent. Her children respect their mother's relationship with her gentleman friend.

Jackie, who has been in a long-distance relationship with a man she has cared about for three years, says, "While visiting him, his 45-year-old daughter snubbed me. She doesn't know me and thinks I'm going to whisk her father away from her. The mother has been gone 11 years. I have my own money and am not a money-hunting person, we've always shared expenses. Now our relationship is in trouble. If it cools off and if I decide to share my life with someone else, I will make sure kids aren't in the picture."

When children are in the mix

- Tina Tessina, in her book, "The Unofficial Guide to Dating Again," says, "If you really want things to go smoothly, children should not even know you're dating. When you go out, you're going out 'with a friend.' No date should be brought home until you know this is a safe person for your children to know. This takes time, unless you're dating someone you already know, and who is known to your friends. Children should not be your confidants. Use your adult friends for that."

- Before moving-in together, a couple needs discuss children issues, and what each person expects. Put your agreement in writing. Deciding not to move-in together is much easier than someone having to move out later

- For the person moving in, don't be naïve thinking you can handle anything and you'll just overlook the baggage (kids, for example) your new mate brings into the relationship. Bliss wears off and reality settles in fairly quickly

- You won't be able to sleep-in late and spur-of-the-moment intimacy is restricted, and there will be extra demands on your time

- For the person with children, before allowing someone to move in, and become your savior, baby-sitter, financier, and bank, keep in mind the children are your responsibility and don't expect someone to become an instant mom or dad and put up with all of the grief kids can dish out. You're the one who had the children, not your partner. She or he is there to help, but not to be the panacea

- Don't let adult children interfere with your life. Kids should want you to be happy, but oftentimes they don't see it that way. They can be selfish, and don't want to lose their inheritance, or they think you're dating too soon, or that you've forgotten mom, and can cause trouble in your relationship

- For adult children, whose parents are trying to date, be supportive. Your parent(s) have the right to pursue a happy life. Don't be selfish. In her book, *Young at Heart,* author Rachelle Zukerman says, "Adult children's negativity contributes to tension between themselves and their parents."

The last thought

Children living at home must be the top priority. Whether a dating couple can function happily under that umbrella depends on a number of factors, with each person's patience and understanding being the biggest factor. The person without children must be willing to give and usually get less in return.

Perhaps, the payoff comes after the kids leave--when the couple can give full attention to each other, that is, if they're still speaking.

Or, perhaps an even bigger payoff comes later when children return home for a visit and thank the step-parent for his or her efforts in helping to raise them. Knowing you made a sacrifice and it was appreciated may be the only reward you need.

It takes a special pair to ride out the children-years together and emerge as a happy, successful couple. But it can be done.

Chapter 16

Honesty and Commitment

You wonder about guys. Now that I've turned 50, it's not like I've got unlimited time to figure them out. Do you think sodium pentathol and a lie detector test are too much for a first date?

--- *a single nurse*

Middle-age dating should be easy. Two lonely people have a date, they determine if they're compatible and enjoy being together, and if so, they start building a loving, meaningful relationship. If not, they thank each other and simply move on. That's how easy it should be.

However, most of the time, it doesn't work out that way. Too often, honesty is an issue. People lie and play games, they say they'll do one thing and don't. Or, others want a relationship instantly. In this chapter, five things mature singles shouldn't have to deal with are discussed, which in the real world, make courtship difficult.

Honesty

The most important characteristic in dating is honesty. If two people are honest, trust is established. Besides, it's easier to be honest than to figure out a good alibi.

--Keith Stroud, age 66, author, retired school principal

The first story comes from Wayne, age 54. After being married twice for a total of 30 years, he became single three years ago and has been dating for about a year. Wayne says, "The problem hasn't been finding charming ladies to date, but the manner in which each must be handled."

Wayne has dated women aged 28 to 52 and says he has learned from each experience. "I've unintentionally hurt some, made others angry, and never heard back from the rest," says Wayne (probably the 28-year-old he had no business dating). He adds that he's made some misjudgments, but he's learned an important lesson about dating, the need to be honest.

He wants to date, learn, and enjoy different experiences, but *he doesn't want to settle down.* He now realizes that he must make his position clear to women before he dates them a second time.

He's found if he dates some women more than twice, they start thinking, "exclusive relationship," hoping for something different than what he wants, which throws the relationship out of sync early. It's happened to him twice.

When he first started dating, one woman perceived the relationship as love and was deeply hurt when told otherwise. Wayne is a sensitive and caring man, and he doesn't want that to happen again.

Wayne says if the right woman comes along, he could change his no-settling-down position, but his honesty stance will remain the same.

Not all singles are as honest as Wayne. People think if they're honest they will hurt the other person's feelings, so they take the cowardly way out, and lie or act deviously. But as Keith Stroud pointed out, being honest is easier than being dishonest.

Some people think being honest about their height, weight or age will hurt their chances of getting a date. They may be right, but when they misrepresent themselves, and then they meet the other person, the truth comes out, and they don't go out again anyway. Everybody's time was wasted.

Bill Buckley, of Gulf Shores, Alabama, said, "I've found dishonesty on the Internet with women, some dating multiple men at the same time. I traveled a long distance to meet a woman, and found she wasn't who she said she was (had misrepresented herself). I took her to dinner only to learn she was still in love with a former lover. It wasted her time and mine."

Honesty would make the middle-age dating world a simpler place. Wayne discovered an added bonus: "I have found some incredible friendships from being honest."

If someone is dishonest with you, they aren't the right person for you. You wouldn't want to be with someone you couldn't trust. True, it's competitive out there, but never sacrifice your principles or honesty for the sake of getting a date.

Games

I've been divorced 15 years. Why do men feel they have to play stupid games?

--woman looking for a straight shooter

Unfortunately, there will always be game players out there. Best to avoid them. We're too old for games. Playing dating games wastes time and energy. Games aren't productive. Everybody loses. We need to conserve our energy just to live and to make our relationships the best they can be.

Yo-yo relationships are games

A yo-yo relationship is where you're pulled toward a person and then pushed away and then pulled back--again and again--at the whim of the person on the other end. One woman said, "I dated a man who professed love, I was happy. Then, he'd distance himself by saying he had changed and didn't have those feelings. When I started dating others, he would chase me. He recently pulled this for the third time. It was a game. I refuse to see him again."

Being in a yo-yo relationship is unhealthy—you're stressed, stomach in knots, never knowing what's coming next. You don't like what you're going through, but it's hard to break away because you care and hope things will change. Human nature can distort reality—we tend to want what we can't have, and we put the elusive person on an unrealistic pedestal.

If you're involved in a yo-yo relationship, and you're the whirling dervish at the end of the string, regain control of your life, and emotions. Begin living again, cut the yo-yo string. Just do it and move on. Don't look back. The longer you wait, the harder it will be to act.

Why don't men call or women respond (when they say they will)?

"I'll call you." When are women going to realize the shallowness of those words and treat them as such? Never depend on someone using those words. The next time someone says they'll call you, smile and tell them goodbye.

--a woman commenting in my "Dating After 50" discussion forum on thirdage.com

There's no rule that says, after having a date, either the man or the woman is required to announce his or her intentions about a second date. No one owes anybody an explanation. Usually, if either wants to go out again, he or she will mention something like, "I had a great time. I hope we can do it again soon."

However, one or both may not know if they'll go out with the person again. Perhaps they have to think about it or perhaps other matters of a higher priority come up that have to be addressed.

Or, a man or woman may have no intention of going out with that person again. In that case, it would be nice to know. A courteous, simple statement like, "I enjoyed your company, but I don't think we'd work out" would be appropriate. But, many daters aren't courteous and could care less about somebody's else's feelings.

Some intend to go out again, but they've read books on dating rules that tell them they must play it cool for awhile and keep the person guessing. This way of thinking falls under the games category and isn't necessary at our age.

I'm not advising making some big deal out of announcing your intentions either way, but common courtesy and respect for others go a long way in dating and in life.

Others are afraid of hurting another's feelings so they feel that saying nothing works best for them. One woman said, "Men use the words 'I will call you' like we use the words, 'See you later.' Men don't like emotional scenes so they just say they'll call, even if they don't plan to."

Some men feel it's a slap in the face to the woman to tell her they aren't interested, and most men don't want to incur the wrath of a woman in person.

I set up Jack on two blind dates. He met one of the women for coffee. Later, he e-mailed her this message: "I had a nice afternoon with you. I do not want to pursue a romantic connection. I would rather be candid than render to you any romantic hope." A little on the blunt side--but honest. At least she knew how he felt and wouldn't harbor hope that he'd call her.

If you have no intention of seeing a person again, and he or she seems interested in you, be honest and tell the person you don't feel it would work out and thank him or her for the time. How hard is that? Treat others as you'd like to be treated.

If it happens to you, don't take it personally. You wouldn't want to be with someone who doesn't want to be with you. Remember, dating at middle age is a numbers game. You may need to date several different people before you find somebody compatible.

Slow down, you're moving too fast

I've never known a woman who thought one-night stands were fun.

--Anne, Aliso Viejo, Calif.

When some people become single, they are in too much of a hurry to get involved again. They think opportunity will pass them by. They've got to find somebody right now. They come off as being desperate, which is a turnoff, as we said in chapter 3.

When dating after losing a mate, take it slowly. Sometimes, we're so lonely and desperate to be loved we try to speed relationships along. We commit too soon, sleep together too soon, move-in too soon, or marry too soon. Then, before we know it, we realize we've made a mistake because we didn't take our time. Tomorrow will come with or without a mate (which could be a blessing). And speaking of moving slowly, some middle age guys take it so slowly they'll never commit.

Why Middle Age Men Won't Commit (And What To Do About It)

A woman asked, "Why do single men, over age 50, not want a commitment? Is this a California thing? Are there just too many women? Do men hang on until something better comes along, and then move on to the next vulnerable woman?"

Seven reasons why men avoid commitment

1. They haven't healed from losing a former love. In Chapter 2, we mentioned the importance of healing before getting involved again. Maybe the guy needs more time

2. Fear. "I'm scared about marriage. Been burned before, and just cannot tolerate the prospect of the pain of divorce again," says Bill Buckley, of Gulf Shores, Alabama.

Some men are leery because of what happened before, they were hurt or taken in their divorce, or had a bad experience. They don't want to risk going through it again

3. Some won't commit because they simply don't want or need to. They're happy with their lives the way they are. By committing, they would give up their freedom

4. Some feel they aren't with the right woman (ouch!) Could be for a variety of reasons. Perhaps they see something about a person they don't like, or they just feel they aren't compatible. Maybe they're too set in their single ways, or maybe they just don't love the woman enough

5. Others prefer the hunt, and don't want a commitment. Once they've made the conquest, they go looking for other game to chase. They'll never be happy with one person

6. Some feel too rushed or pressured. They feel smothered. They may need more time, and less pressure

7. Some want the benefits of a relationship, but not the responsibilities that go along with a commitment. Sort of the "why-buy-the-cow when-the-milk-is-free?" way of thinking. They reason, why give up a good thing?

Dealing with men who won't commit

When your guy won't commit, have a talk. Find out what he's thinking and why he's reluctant. Once you've gathered the facts, you can make the decision whether or not you think he'll change, and whether or not you'll hang around.

If you feel he needs time—and he's worth it to you--give him lots of freedom, air to breath, and treat him well. Don't rush or push him. Appreciate and enjoy your own freedom. Let him decide when he's ready.

If he keeps backing off, and won't commit, and the weeks turn into months (even years), and if commitment is so important to you, you may need to let him go. Why be with somebody who doesn't want to be with you?

The longer you allow the situation to drag on, the harder terminating the relationship will be. And, you're losing opportunity time to meet someone else.

Understand, if you say goodbye, he'll likely be gone forever. Be sure you're prepared for that. Allow him back into your life only on your terms--with a commitment. In the next chapter, we shed more light on whether to stay in a relationship or move on.

Dishonesty, games, saying one thing, doing another, not wanting to commit, deciding to stay or leave a relationship, are all a part of middle-age dating. It would be nice if you didn't have to deal with those issues, but chances are you will, and it's best if you're prepared.

Chapter 17

A Tough Call: Ending a Relationship

It took me forever to leave my husband. I was afraid I'd never find anyone who'd want to go out with me. My expectations of him being the man of my dreams blinded me to his abusive personality.

--a 44-year-old divorcee from Santa Fe

The major part of this book has focused on how to meet someone. But there are many people over 50 who are in relationships that aren't working. They don't know what to do. Should they stay or leave? It's an agonizing decision.

From time to time, readers ask me if they should end a relationship. That's a tough call, and not in my job description to advise them. It depends on so many factors. Staying together is better, if two parties can work things out.

It may be time to end it when:

- You've had enough of any of a number of things, but being treated poorly tops the list. Being mentally or physically abused, put down, yelled at, criticized or not appreciated fall under that umbrella

- You're no longer willing to wait for the relationship to change and get better, hoping someday you'll be happy

- Either one of you has stopped caring about the other

- You're tired of trying to convince the person you're worthy of him or her

- You're in a relationship and lonely

- All of your efforts to improve the situation--discussions, communication and counseling--have failed

- You've stayed together only for the children, and now they're gone

- You keep making excuses for your mate's unacceptable behavior

- You've been told too often "It's my way or the highway"

- You're afraid to talk fearing another fight will follow

- You give but don't receive, and know you deserve better. Rod, in Dallas, said, "It hurts not getting back what you give."

- You realize by not taking action, you're missing out on the opportunity to build a new life.

One woman wrote, "I got the big rush at the beginning of a relationship. I felt we had similar goals about where the relationship was heading. Then, that dreaded conversation about the future and no promises. I was kept 'on the hook' for almost a year. Losing him? Ha! I was only losing a 'part' of him. He had many good qualities, but treating me well wasn't one of them."

Sandy, San Jose, Calif., said, "Tensions that came with the relationship were not healthy. I just believed that the potential was real and good—and overlooked that it was an unending 'convincing' job to have him see it that way. Being close should be a natural joy—it wasn't."

It won't be easy

Neil Sedaka had a number one hit in 1961, called, *Breaking Up Is Hard To Do.* That still rings true today. Even if you initiate the decision, letting go won't be easy. It doesn't mean you stop caring. Country group Little Texas has a song called, *Love Doesn't Stop on a Dime.* It doesn't, you just don't turn off the love faucet. Don't think your life is going to be wonderful just because you're free.

Walking away from a lover or spouse may be the hardest thing you ever do. It takes guts to say, "This is going to hurt, but we'll be better off in the long run." Letting go may be the only way for both parties to seek better lives. Some couples aren't compatible, they just can't get along, or their love is gone. Their relationships are stormy, perhaps even dangerous.

One last try

If you truly care about each other, give it another chance. Staying in a relationship is easier for both (if you can work it out) than going it alone. Try counseling. When you separate, you give up the benefits you've built together—

sharing expenses, one home, one mortgage. But, if the feelings are gone, gone, gone, then, it's time to go.

When to end it?

Tina Tessina says, "One mistake I see women make frequently is to put too much significance on certain indicators of love. It's worthwhile to step back from your focus on what you're "not" getting and take a look at what you "are" getting. If you can have pleasant companionship with someone who's kind and nice to you, perhaps you should make sure you're not cutting of your nose to spite your face. Any woman has to make this choice for herself, but I recommend weighing the pros and cons of this relationship against the pros and cons of being alone. Happiness often means settling for 80% of what you want, instead of 100%. The key is knowing whether staying together is worth it or not."

Only you will know when it's time to go, when instinct tells you. You may have thought about it for years. Then, one day you just decide.

Don't wait to go until you've got a replacement and don't let a replacement trigger the decision. As we learned in chapter 2, we need time to heal after a loss.

The holidays are peak times for ending relationships because people take stock during the holidays and make New Year's resolutions to improve their lives. Evaluating a relationship is often one of the items on the check-off list. If you get the holiday itch to make your decision, perhaps wait a month or two to be sure you weren't dealing with just a holiday surge of emotions.

My third marriage ended on Xmas Eve, I didn't know it was coming. My first marriage ended on January 1. In the latter case, my wife and I had agreed that we'd start a new year with our new lives. It made those holidays awful-- opening presents on Xmas Day when you knew in a week you were going separate ways forever.

After the breakup

Lynda Thompson, of Huntington Beach, Calif., e-mailed, "After the first few weeks, the pain of being out of it was so much less than the pain of being in it, I knew I had done the right thing." Lynda's experience is what often happens when a relationship we're in ends.

One woman said: "My marriage broke up after 35 years. He left for a 22-year-old who was after him for a green card and his Rolex®. The joke's on him. I look fantastic, have my family, get half the money, and he is old, tired, and has the most important things in his life gone: his real family and a new grandbaby that he always wanted."

And this is how that same woman felt a year later, "I haven't fully recovered from the hurt…my feelings towards the ex are that of sadness and pity…I have more empathy and love towards people…I like myself and enjoy my time with me…my spirituality has grown…I'm seeing light at the end of the tunnel…it has been a long, frightful journey."

When relationships end, we tend to look back and wonder if only I had done this or that, perhaps it could have been salvaged. It's doubtful. We tend to forget the bad and remember the good. Don't look back. You had the guts to make a decision, now have the guts to live it and grow. But, do everything possible to save it before going.

Chapter 18

Preparing to be single

I'm with my spouse because I am foolishly dependent upon him. I never took the time to seriously think about getting a job or establishing my own independence. I let him talk me into staying home and that is what is happening to me. I have nothing and am 52, and starting very late

--A Long Island, NY housewife

Over the last nine years of writing my columns, I've heard from many widows who are totally lost after losing their spouses. They never learned to balance a checkbook, drive a car, or to develop their own hobbies or interests or make decisions. They have no idea of where to begin or how to function in life. For some, when their spouses die, they in effect, die with them. I've added this short chapter to help them.

Most singles can breeze right through this chapter. So can people who are in relationships *and* who have interests, friends, and "a life" outside of those relationships.

This chapter is for the person like the woman quoted above, so dependent on her husband, if she becomes single, she'll be lost. She admits at age 52 she has nothing. What a terrible position to be in, married or single. She needs to start making a life for herself, to grow and learn to stand on her own.

This chapter is not about preparing oneself to date or re-enter the dating scene. Nor is it about preparing oneself to lessen the hurt of a loss—we can never prepare for that.

It's about preparing oneself to be independent enough to stand on one's own two feet, if one has to face the world alone. When we become stronger as individuals, it should strengthen our marriages and relationships. And, by being better prepared, if we ever lose our spouse or partner, it should help us survive and cope better.

What can people do while they are in a happy, wonderful, loving and fulfilling relationship to better prepare themselves to cope with life--should they lose their spouse or significant other--without diminishing the relationship? Some people are horrified at the thought.

Glenda said, "The entire concept of preparing for the end of a relationship without hurting that relationship is ludicrous! The 'preparing' delivers the lethal blow."

Alexis, 53, sided with Glenda, "When it hurts it hurts, and there isn't much anyone can do about it. It's like going for an operation, how do you prepare?"

Elliott Ryal, 63, added, "There's no preparation to be on your own while still loving your mate."

Books, therapists, columnists, church professionals, and others dispense advice to help people *after* a loss. Some readers shared what they would have done differently *before* their loss to make it easier to cope.

Most feel preparing is important

Jim Rue, 52, Laguna Beach, Calif., said, "Maintain friendships outside of the relationship. In the past, I've let friends go when awkwardness between a friend and a new partner occurred, never again."

What would Barbara Gilvary, Laguna Hills, Calif., have done differently? "I would have made sure I could support myself, worked on my bachelor's or master's degree, and kept closer ties with my family and friends. I would have 'allowed' my ex the same."

Suzy Olson, Mission Viejo, Calif., said: "True love, forever, is wonderful, but, I would have been a less submissive wife and taken better care of me."

Burl Estes, also of Mission Viejo, says he knows of a woman turning 50 who is floundering. "She's facing the prospect of having to get a full-time job, and of starting to plan for retirement." Burl feels if she hadn't wasted years of insisting on being taken care of, and focused on personal development, she would have been better prepared.

"You absolutely MUST have your own life. If you center everything around the 'we' of the relationship, then you lose everything when it's over. Now that I don't require a partner, I'm happier, and when I meet someone, he'll know I'm not the clingy type," says Irene, Laguna Hills, Calif.

Doug Spoors made a valid point, "The least prepared person would be the most dependent on the other, which isn't conducive to a good relationship. Being prepared may improve a present relationship."

Lynda Thompson, Huntington Beach, Calif., advised: "Keep at least one credit card and checking account solely in your name. Be aware of joint accounts. My husband took my name off all of our credit cards and checking and savings accounts when we separated. It was extremely difficult--no home, money or credit, only my car (fortunately in my name). After a breakup, you have no idea what the 'wonderful man' you married may become or do."

Betty, 63, says she wishes she had been more involved in groups, volunteering, church, hobbies, sports (golf, tennis) and computer class. She said when people are in a bad relationship, they tend not to have friends.

A Rockwall, Texas, woman said, "I was a stay-at-home mom, devoting everything to the kids, house and his parents. I had nothing for myself outside of those interests. It has been a painful growing period, but I see now that I was responsible for things being so lop-sided for me."

Jeanne Fleming, Murray, Kentucky, says, "People in marriages need to be prepared and maintain some independence. When I was married, I was certain nothing would happen to the marriage, but it did. We grow too soon old, and too late smart."

One woman's situation is an example of why people need to be more independent. Jean, 63, Murietta, Calif, was married 43 years. Her ex-husband worked for an employer with a private pension. She stayed home and raised children. Now divorced, she has no social security, and pays for health insurance. If her ex dies, she won't qualify for his pension. To receive social security, she'll have to work until she's 72. Too bad she didn't start planning earlier.

Granted, preparing to be single can be a sticky issue, but shouldn't be. Most enlightened people feel having friends, money, and interests--independent of their mates-- is wise. The key is not too much separateness. It's like the concept of life insurance, preparing for any eventuality. I recommend reading, "How To Be A Couple and Still Be Free," by Tina Tessina, for a professional's insight.

Chapter 19

Being Single Isn't So Bad

I've come to treasure my times alone. Someday, I hope to settle down again....but I'm not in any hurry, and lately, I've found I'm "ok" with being single for the rest of my life. Dating and being single in my forties has been quite a journey. I'm loving it!

--Robin Nugent, 46 Buena Park, Calif.

In the United States, there are approximately 33 million singles over the age of 45. Many are lonely and would like to have a mate. But not all. Some think being single isn't so bad, in fact, it's the life they choose. People should be careful for what they wish, they may just get it in the form of a mate. And then they find out they were better off single. Not all mid-life relationships are made in heaven. Several women shared their reasons for remaining single.

Dolores Williams, Temecula, Calif., said: "I've been married and unhappy, and single and unhappy, and single and unhappy is better." Not many of us would argue with Dolores.

Lisa, Costa Mesa, Calif., didn't mince words. "I prefer to be single," she said, "because I already have a job, and I don't need two." Sounds like Lisa believes men are too much work

Alexis has dates but hasn't found anybody who's right for her. "I'm about ready to give up on dating. I can't find what I want. Thank God I got rid of the last two. It's better to be alone, than to be with someone you don't want to be with. So, here I am, alone again."

DeAnne Hine, of San Clemente, Calif, says, "When you're a single woman, you don't have to worry about falling into the toilet in the middle of the night because the seat is up." Suggestion for DeAnne: If your man doesn't put the seat down, install a night light in the bathroom and keep him around. (I heard a man is working on an invention that automatically returns the toilet seat down. He calls it, "the relationship saver.)

And, there's the squeezing-of-the toothpaste-in-the-middle complaint from women. Now they've even got gadgets you can turn to keep the toothpaste flowing, so that's no longer a good reason for remaining single.

Angie Jarrett, Dana Point, Calif., says she's a contented single: "I love men, without them we wouldn't have a world. But I'm fine not having one. It's what you make of life, and put into it that matters. Help yourself first."

"Many of my lady friends are satisfied being single, widowed and living alone. They don't have to cook, clean, or do laundry for anyone, or share their money or their home." said, Jean Wendelsdorf, Orange, Calif.

Another said, "I never knew real happiness until I got married, by then it was too late."

A woman from Amarillo, Texas, said, "I'm a 51-year-old divorcee, single for 13 years. I love my single life, and it will take an extraordinary man to convince me to change.

Three women who likely won't marry again

A woman named Fran, who described herself as "49 and holding," said, "I prefer and am happily content, in the last third of my life, to be single. There is a difference in being alone and in being lonely. When you have comparatively good health, varied interests, a few close friends with whom you can share the pleasures life offers, and the financial security to do those things that bring you joy, there's no need to feel lonely or to remarry. For many of us, the privacy and control of our own lives is a welcomed change from the demands of previous years. We've 'been there, done that,' and 'paid our dues.'"

And this from a woman in Richmond, Kentucky: "I haven't met anyone for a long time with whom I'm compatible. I don't get lonely because I'm accustomed to doing a lot of activities alone and with friends. I don't want someone requiring a lot of my free time. I don't want to marry again nor live with a guy, but I do miss the kissing and hugging."

Lisa: "I've been single for 12 years and love it. I don't have time to feel sorry for myself. Most good, moral men with any quality are still committed to their wives. I'm not interested in second-hand men who couldn't make it in their first or second marriage—that's a problem waiting to happen." (Since Lisa was married before, doesn't that make her a second-hand woman?)

Happy being single but...

"I've been widowed for 12 years, after being married to the same great guy for 27 years," said Joanne Herbel, Fountain Valley, Calif., "I think it's great being single. I come and go whenever and wherever I want. I answer to no one. I eat what I want, when I want. I pick up and clean up after me only. I don't miss having to worry about someone else. All that aside, I'd trade in all my wonderful freedom if I found someone I fell in love with, and who fell in love with me. But I'm not out there desperately searching. If it happens—fine."

Sandi shared: "I was married for 20 years, and have now been unmarried for 18. It took awhile for me to see that being single was not a bad thing. I like having the freedom to come and go as I please. Being divorced has taught me to depend on myself. I can dine and travel alone. I have some wonderful women friends, and like to spend time with them, but I crave alone time.

"I would like to date, but just haven't met anyone. So I guess I would find myself in the category of being comfortable with being single, rather than preferring it. When I look at some married couples, I'm glad I'm single."

Pat from Jacksonville, Florida, said: "I'm a 53-year-old woman who is starting over after many years of marriage. My husband found the grass greener in everyone else's backyard, so now he has the house, and I have my sanity."

Wendie, Long Island, NY, said: "When I became single, I tried to heal my wounds, thinking another head on the pillow to replace the one that left would complete me again. After several incompatible relationships, I'm taking a breather. I was programmed from my earliest years to think that life was worth living only if one had a boyfriend, or a husband. Not true."

Three Goats?

And to end this chapter, of all the reasons to remain single, my favorite was mailed to me years ago by a woman who opted not to sign her letter. Too bad, I've always wanted to give her credit. She wrote: "Living with a man would be like having three goats in the house."

So, it's come to that? We men are considered goats? Remember, being single isn't so bad.

Chapter 20

Remember To Dance

There's been a wealth of information presented in this book to help you find love after 50.

Here are the nine most important points to remember.

1. Be yourself. Be natural. Don't worry about rules or whether you should do this or that. Be honest, even when others aren't

2. Protect your heart, health, assets and wine glass. Beware when meeting strangers. Don't be gullible or naïve

3. No partner is worth causing you unhappy tears, only happy tears. If someone doesn't love you the way you want them to, it doesn't mean they don't love you with all they have

4. Don't waste your time on a partner who isn't willing to waste his or her time on you

5. Get off the couch, out of the house and out among people. Pursue outside activities and interests you enjoy. Go out for you, to revitalize your life, to make you a better person

6. Don't overlook networking. It's the least expensive and most effective date-finding tool. Be friendly, approachable, positive and open to making new acquaintances

7. Don't expect someone else to fix your life

8. Be patient, considerate and gentle. Have fun. Enjoy life. And when you least expect it, when you aren't looking, someone special will enter it. Don't let loneliness drive your decisions

9. Remember to dance. Pick yourself up, and get out there.

Recommended Books To Read

Boundaries in Dating	Drs. Cloud & Townsen
Chicken Soup For The Grieving Soul	
	Mark Victor Hansen Jack Canfield
How To Be A Couple and Still Be Free	Tina Tessina, Ph.D
Mars And Venus Starting Over	John Gray, Ph.D
Master Dating: How to Meet & Attract Quality Men!	Felicia Rose Adler
The Five Love Languages	Gary Chapman
The One Minute Millionaire	Mark Victor Hansen Robert G. Allen
The Ten Smartest Decisions Woman Can Make After Forty	Tina Tessina, Ph.D
The Unofficial Guide to Dating Again	Tina Tessina, Ph.D
Young At Heart	Rachelle Zukerman, Ph.D

154

Index

About the Author

Tom Blake is a columnist for *The Orange County Register* in southern California. He has written more than 500 newspaper columns on middle-age dating and relationships, and has appeared on the *Today* show as a dating after 50 expert.

Tom has owned Tutor and Spunky's Deli for 15 years, a bustling gathering-spot on Pacific Coast Highway in Dana Point, Calif., where couples have met and dating stories flourish. Tom met his life partner, Greta Cohn, when she came into his deli and ordered a carrot juice.

Tom is a motivational speaker. He spoke at the national AARP convention in San Diego in 2002, and will speak at the national AARP convention in Chicago in 2003.

Tom is the host of an online forum called "Dating After 50" (www.thirdage.com). His columns are featured on msn.com.

His book, "Middle Aged and Dating Again," (Tooter's Publishing, 1997, revised 2001), is a humorous account of his first year of dating after his third divorce. The book had a second printing in 2001.

During his varied career, Tom has worked for the Irving Trust Company (a Wall Street bank); American Airlines, Trans World Airlines; Victoria Station (the boxcar-themed restaurant chain of the 1970s); The Oakland Invaders football team of the USFL; and various computer companies.

To receive Tom's weekly column by e-mail, contact him at TPBlake@aol.com, or write to him at P.O. Box 442, Dana Point, Calif., 92629.

His website is www.tooterspublishing.com.

A native of Jackson, Michigan, Tom has a Master's Degree in business from The University of Michigan and a BA degree from DePauw University, Greencastle, Indiana. He and Greta live in San Clemente, Calif.

Order Sheet

To order additional copies of *Finding Love After 50. How to Begin. Where to Go. What to Do,* complete the information below.

Ship to (please print):

Name_____

Address_____

City_____

State_____ Zip_____

_____copies @ $17.95 each $_____

Postage and handling $4.00 (1-3 books) $_____

$5.00 (4-plus books) $_____

California residents add 7.75% sales tax $_____

Total amount enclosed $_____

Make checks payable to: **Tooter's Publishing** and mail to

Tutor and Spunky's Deli
34135 Pacific Coast Highway
Dana Point, CA 92629

For telephone or credit card orders: 949 248-9008

e-mail: TPBlake@aol.com